MAKE IT HAPPEN

Make It Happen

Every Woman's Guide to Balancing Career & Family

Elizabeth Bialow Magazine

Published by Game Changer Publishing

Paperback ISBN: 978-1-965653-13-5
Hardcover ISBN: 978-1-965653-14-2
Digital ISBN: 978-1-965653-15-9

GC | GAME CHANGER
PUBLISHING

www.GameChangerPublishing.com

DEDICATION

This book is dedicated to my parents, Linda and Martin Bialow, without whom I could not make anything happen in my life.

Read This First

Just to say thanks for buying and reading my book, I would like to give you a free video about personal branding, no strings attached!

SCAN THE QR CODES

@elizabethmagazineesq   LawthenticConsulting.com

MAKE IT HAPPEN

Every Woman's Guide to Balancing Career & Family

Elizabeth Bialow Magazine

GC GAME CHANGER PUBLISHING

www.GameChangerPublishing.com

FOREWORD

Elizabeth Magazine's *Make It Happen* is filled with anecdotes and advice for "Everywoman"—a.k.a. every woman who has ever dared to dream, faced obstacles but pressed on, and to every woman who believes that her voice, her ideas, and her passion for creating a life you love can shape the world.

This book is a must-read for all the trailblazers, visionaries, and everyday heroines who make it happen, one step at a time.

I have had the privilege of having a front-row seat to the author's life and every chapter of this book. Elizabeth is my older sister, mentor, and best friend. She has blazed a trail and lit up every room she ever entered. She has the confidence every woman wants and a belief in herself that is contagious. She is beauty and power mixed with grace under pressure.

Her challenges of balancing motherhood as a working woman are the same for many of us. The difference with her journey is how she handles the bumps in the road. She is a risk-taker and quick decision-maker. She doesn't ruminate. She can change the course of her ship in moments. But those are most often the moments that matter.

As a child, when my mother sent us both into a store to buy milk, Elizabeth would direct me to speak to the cashier because she was too shy. But she had no issue telling me to do it. Her "Boss Babe" mentality started young and took her places. There was never a doubt in her mind that she would find success.

She showed me the way as a mother and a professional. Everything I did, from joining the dance team in high school to a sorority in college, was because her footsteps were the ones I wanted to follow. As a mother, she taught me the "right way" to change a diaper, clip the baby's nails, and schedule feeding times. Her tips on how to make it happen at home and work are invaluable.

It has taken me 50+ years of watching her path on these trails to fully understand her. Her seize-the-day, morning coffee buzz, get-it-done mentality works. But now, as she is entering the stage of life where reflection has become just as much of a priority as moving fast, she has taken a pause to put her legacy knowledge in this book so you can all benefit from her advice.

— *Jennifer Zeidler*

TABLE OF CONTENTS

INTRODUCTION

66 ────────────────────

"You can make your goals in life happen if you put the hard work in and believe that you can accomplish anything."

──────────────────── **99**

Are you exhausted and burning the candle at both ends? Do you feel like there is not enough time in the day to get everything done? Do you have an endless to-do list that never gets completed? Do you feel like you do not measure up to other women around you? Are you isolated, overwhelmed, and completely paralyzed? Do you want more from your life? Do you want more balance? Do you worry that your marriage is not healthy? Are you struggling to balance career and family? You are not alone.

I am a mother, entrepreneur, lawyer, wife, and consultant. I founded, launched, and successfully exited two companies that I grew from startups to multimillion-dollar businesses. I raised $40 million to start a business, then scaled and sold that company in less than five

1

years. Currently, I am the founder of a consulting business and help business owners enhance their personal and professional brands with social media. At this stage of my life, I focus on unwinding, finding peace in the simplest of moments, working on my relationships, and helping others achieve balance while juggling work, life, and family. I wrote this book to share my story and offer you tips about how you can make anything in your life possible while still protecting your peace and achieving a healthy level of balance.

This book will take you on a journey where I will incorporate my personal experiences, challenges, and successes at various stages of life. I will provide advice and a blueprint for you to thrive. This book is a guide for every woman striving for balance. If you are a career woman in your 20s this book will help you form habits for the future. If you are an exhausted wife and mother trying to figure out how to work and have a fulfilling career while raising your children without having a breakdown, this book will guide you. If you are married and struggling with the relationship, I provide resources to help your marriage. If you are contemplating divorce, I provide advice about this difficult decision. Finally, if you are an empty nester in midlife embarking on the next chapter and feeling lonely while yearning to go back to work, I will give you advice about this stage of life and work on how to make it the prime time of your life. I will also outline how to create a robust personal brand to reinvent yourself.

You will be able to utilize this book as a roadmap for success and will learn that anything in life is possible. You *can* make things happen in your life while preserving balance and finding joy. I will share the secrets of my success in both my work and personal life. I want you to learn from my successes and also from the difficulties I encountered along the way. The evolution and growth that occurred while I was figuring it all out gave me the perspective and life experience to help guide you through the tough times. Come for a ride with me; with perseverance, hard work, and resilience, you can do and have anything you set your mind to.

With perseverance, hard work, and resilience, you can do and have anything you set your mind to.

Make it happen: That is what I told my kids and my sales team every day. When my children asked me about a school project, I would say, "What can you do to make this happen?" When my employees asked for assistance, I would simply say, "If you want the account, what can you do to make it happen?" Soon, my team started putting signs around the office that said, *"Make it happen."* The account executives gifted me with trays and t-shirts with the slogan. We manifested success daily. Is it as simple as that? Of course not. It takes discipline, effort, planning, patience, and perseverance to build a brand and launch a company. However, if you want something badly enough and if you believe you can achieve your goals, then anything is possible, and you can definitely "Make it happen!" The "it" in making it happen is any goal you set your mind to and dream about.

Women have often asked me how I did it all. I raised three smart and accomplished kids, traveled for work several times per month, and led the sales and marketing teams of two successful companies. While parenting, I launched a business with an idea and grew it from a boot-strapped start-up to a successful specialty finance company that sold in less than five years. Wherever I traveled, women were often surprised when I told them that I cooked, entertained, decorated my home, worked out, and spent time with my friends and family. "How do you do it all?" they asked. Many of these conversations happened when I was entertaining executives at business dinners or during breaks from meetings.

Although, on the outside, I appeared to be easily juggling work and family, the reality was often quite different. I called my kids from the bathroom and put my "mom" hat on while simultaneously entertaining my business colleagues at long fancy dinners. It was not easy, and the need to be perfect pushed me to unhealthy levels. My marriage failed along this journey, and this detrimentally affected several aspects of my life. I did not have the traditional happy ending that you read about in books. The more my business thrived, the more my marriage and personal life deteriorated. During the sale of the company, I experienced a painful divorce with my ex-husband, who was also my business partner. With a lot of work and effort, we are now effective co-parents.

I have remarried and have an incredible partner who makes me laugh, motivates me, and lifts me up daily. Finding love with my new husband was only possible after I did a deep dive into my own issues, gained self-awareness, and evolved. We work on our communication and relationship on a daily basis. Laughter has been the anecdote to our struggles. My happy ending took a winding road via some occasional dead ends, twisting paths, and storms along the way. Is it easy? Definitely not! Do I struggle? Absolutely! It takes a village to raise kids and succeed in the competitive business world. I was lucky to have a supportive extended family and friends who helped me through tough times.

Integration of one's family and marriage can work successfully with each other; work and family do not have to be at odds. However, in order to successfully juggle the two it is critical to put strategies and habits into place and to put the work into your relationships before there are issues. Whether you have babies, elementary-aged children, or kids in high school or college, the struggle is real. You will inevitably feel overwhelmed regularly; you will also feel guilty that something you are doing is not being done perfectly. You will feel that you aren't doing enough for your kids, aren't executing properly at work, and aren't putting enough effort into your marriage or yourself. The warning on the airplane from the flight attendants to put your oxygen mask on first so you can help others around you is so true. If you lack healthy balance, then everything around you will fall apart. Forming strong, healthy habits is crucial for work-life balance.

As your story unfolds, weave my story into your own narrative and learn what to do and what not to do along the way. Also, we will explore what happens when the kids leave for college. When you have been working and raising kids for many years and suddenly find yourself with an empty nest—with no more tasks and unlimited time on your hands—what do you do? Is it possible to reinvent yourself? The empty nest is something that should not be minimized. It often comes at a time when you are taking care of aging parents. Also, many adult children are now struggling to launch and move back home. This new phenomenon creates additional challenges during an already complex stage of life. Midlife can be an incredibly painful time for both a busy professional mom who slows down at work and has very little to do at home and a stay-at-home mother whose entire existence was centered around her family. You will redefine this period in your life and learn how you pick up the pieces and market yourself by creating a personal brand.

You may be asking yourself, *Why do I want to read about Elizabeth's story? Who has the time to read about a suburban housewife who worked and raised her children with some struggles along the way?* I appreciate that your time is a precious commodity, and perhaps my life is not the type of salacious story that is a page-turning thriller. However, this is also not a therapeutic diary session. This book is for young professional women at the start of their careers, for women embarking on marriage and making decisions about work and family, and for women in the halftime of their lives who want to rebrand and create a new chapter during midlife and an empty nest. I have reflected on my own story in order to shed light on issues that my friends and I faced. I searched in bookstores and online for a book that had a roadmap for how to thrive and have balance in my life. There were books on each individual topic. However, I could not find a book that took me through all the life stages. I spent years reading about and working on balance, burnout, branding, and relationships. In this book, I have used research from authors who have made a difference in my personal and professional life. This will provide a one-stop book that can guide you through the seasons of your life.

I always knew I would write a book. As a young girl, I aspired to become a writer. I spent years of my childhood reading, writing poetry, authoring short stories, and imagining what my life would eventually look like. I did not know where I would end up. However, I did know that the voyage would be an adventure. I always lived my life with the "glass-half-full" mentality and the adage, "Try it because what is the worst thing that could happen?" I still have that "glass-half-full" philosophy. However, I also now look at life and ask, "What is the best thing that will occur?"

Top 5 Things to Make Your Dreams Happen:

1. Think positively.
2. Ask yourself what is the best thing that can happen.
3. Plan ahead.
4. Be patient.
5. Work hard.

CHAPTER 1

TIME MACHINE: FORMATIVE FOUNDATION

66 ——————————————

"Go back in time and find your 'why.' Your story began with dreaming as a child. Find your inner child and capture the essence of who you are, and your true authentic self will surface."

—————————————— **99**

Buckle up, and let's take a ride together. When you decide to achieve great things in your life, looking back at your past can help you figure out where you want to end up. Looking into the future can help you plan for midlife, which can be redefined as the "prime time" of your life. For the busy "mompreneur" who wants to slow down while still feeling productive, we will learn how to build a personal brand after raising children. However, remember that the only way to find peace is to live in the present. It is okay to look back to learn and to look forward to strategize. Living in the current moment, however, will create a "Zen Zone" around you and help you find peace. In order to find your *why*, and really know yourself, reflect on your childhood and remember who and what you wanted to be when you grew up.

Let's go back to the beginning. The most important relationship in life is the parent-child relationship. My father was a successful cardiologist and medical school professor. My mother had a bachelor's degree from Radcliffe, received a master's degree from Harvard, and taught high school and college English courses. It is daunting to have two Ivy League parents. For me, this was part of my DNA; reading and writing were always passions of mine. SAT words graced the refrigerator doors, and Emily Dickinson was a household name. I grew up with a sister close in age and a younger brother in a close-knit family unit. Lazy days and summers reading everything from biographies of famous presidents to romance novels and all the classics kept me quite busy. These were the days before iPhones, computers, tablets, the Internet, and social media. In the 1970s and early 80s, being present was never something that had to be aspired to. Anxiety was not a word, and stress was not a household discussion. Eye contact was easy because we did not know any different. When someone spoke to us, we focused because there was nothing else to pay attention to or focus on.

The only way to find peace is to live in the present.

So much attention these days focuses on the idea of being in the present moment. Eckhart Tolle's theory in his popular book *The Power of Now*[1] stresses the importance of living in the moment. However, the

[1] Tolle, Eckhart. *The Power of Now*, New World Library, 2001

author also states that the past can play a major role in shaping how we look at the world around us. In today's world, attention is a commodity, as it is difficult to capture. In my family, we sat at the dinner table and discussed the news my parents had read about in the daily newspaper that was delivered to our front lawn. We did not have phones to compete for our attention. When the Vietnam War was raging, my parents shielded us from the carnage by turning the TV off during the nightly news and sending us upstairs to do our homework. We did not worry about a lack of focus because there was nothing else to pay attention to. Music played from record players in the family room and our TV was a shared family appliance. Other than coming home to a bowl of popcorn and an episode of *General Hospital* before starting our homework, there were no devices fighting to take away our attention.

Simple, carefree Florida beach life was the backdrop for my easy-going childhood. I loved school, learning, socializing, dancing, reading, and listening to music. Fast forward to my college years living in New Orleans, attending Tulane University, and then on to law school at the University of Florida, I was on a fast path to success. The reason I decided to attend law school had to do with self-preservation and high school trauma. I watched my best friend, Vicki, get run over by a drunk driver. I left my freshman year at Tulane to travel back to Florida and testify as a key witness at the trial. Her murderer got off because his lawyer was better than the state attorney. After witnessing the incompetence of the prosecutor, I vowed to become a lawyer and seek justice for those less fortunate than I was.

Another impetus for attending law school stemmed from a career day at my sorority. A sorority sister and alum came to speak, and her story mesmerized me. She was a divorced lawyer and a mom who worked part-time. I loved that she had reinvented herself and had a profession to fall back on after her divorce. It was important to me that I was self-sufficient. I remember thinking that I did not want to have a situation where I relied on my husband to be the sole breadwinner. I was afraid that if I relied on a man to provide for me and my future children, we would have no backup plan. I did love a good backup plan!

Clearly, that plan served me well as my life unfolded. After graduation from law school, I accepted my first job at a small law firm in downtown Chicago, practicing workers' compensation law. I was thrown haphazardly into the frenetic pace of the State of Illinois administrative system of red tape and systemized chaos. I learned first-hand the art of negotiation, compromise, relationship building, networking, and sales. I made a very low salary. To make extra money, my boss informed me I needed to bring new cases into the firm. In less than a year, I brought in a considerable amount of business by promoting myself. I authored sections of the Workers' Compensation Law Association journals, scheduled speaking engagements, and set up meetings to educate union members about the newly enacted Americans with Disabilities Act. I met with other referral sources and lawyers and soon built a robust and proliferate referral network. That was all at the ripe age of 26–28 years.

When I became pregnant with my first son, Andrew, everything changed. In the early 1990s, women were not considered valuable in some spheres of work after pregnancy. On one frigid below-zero day, I walked pregnant through downtown Chicago from the train station to my law office. While walking over the iced-over bridge, I slipped and fell backward with my massive down parka acting as a cushion and slid like a large seal across the icy bridge. Tearful, rattled, and frazzled, I confronted my boss. I insisted on a more flexible work schedule, or I would have to resign. He calmly informed me that resignation would be the best option. He basically fired a six-month pregnant woman for asking for flexibility to work from home. I left my fast-paced downtown law firm career to be a stay-at-home mom for my firstborn.

The decision to become a stay-at-home mother was easy at that time, as my boss did not give me the option to stay and work. There is a poignant book about making the choice to be a stay-at-home mother: *The Stay-at-Home Survival Guide: Field-Tested Strategies for Staying Smart, Sane, and Connected While Caring for Your Kids* by Melissa Stanton provides advice about how to make this difficult and most important decision. Social, emotional, and financial factors all need to be considered when deciding to stay home. Today, it is almost impossible to make this choice as the cost of living has increased substantially, and most parents need double incomes in order to support their families and prepare for the future.

It is important to embrace your upbringing and reflect on your own childhood in order to understand your passions and values when determining your career path and making decisions about staying at home with your children. Use your personal challenges to help you navigate adversity and find your passion. These experiences will build your resilience and independently foster a career and life plan that will enable you to find your purpose. Just as I used my experiences to become a lawyer in order to right wrongs and to provide me with a backup plan for my family, you can use your own story to find your career and life path. Life often demands flexibility, especially when balancing career aspirations with family responsibilities.

Use your personal challenges to help you navigate adversity and find your passion.

Throughout this book, I would like you to journal about your own story and strategize about your personal brand. You are the author of your own life story and you can enhance and build your personal brand in many ways. Travel back in time and reflect on your childhood to help you make decisions about the present. Work-life balance is achieved when you can prioritize personal well-being and multitask family responsibilities, even if this means making difficult career choices. Most couples no longer have the luxury of choosing for either partner to stay at home with the children. However, work-from-home schedules and the Family Medical Leave Act mandates have allowed couples to share the workload in the home while both parents work. At the end of the day, my biggest accomplishment is my three children. They are smart, hardworking, and creative. I cannot wait to see where life takes them, and I am excited about my eventual new role as a grandmother. Always keep in mind that your family is more important than any award, career accomplishment, or promotion.

When I look back, I realize that so much of who I am has to do with the way I grew up. Specifically, the people you surround yourself with will influence your life and decision making. Life does not happen in a vacuum. Although being present is an admirable goal, you need to look back to understand your *why*. To fully evolve, it is necessary to review your past traumas to heal and see how these experiences shape who you are now. Your role as a spouse, parent, sibling, friend, and boss all stem from your childhood.

The relationships you build with people throughout your life journey are a reflection on who you are and how you evolve.

Find the time while you are on this journey to make things happen, and true personal growth will occur. Give your full attention to this project. The time you spend working on yourself now will help you in the future.

Why It Is Important to Look Back on Your Childhood:

1. Reflection will help you keep your family as the priority.
2. Childhood dreams will allow you to find your current passion and build your personal brand.
3. Remembering all of life's challenges will make you more self-aware and build your emotional intelligence.
4. Who you are today is a reflection of how you grew up.
5. Bringing back that childhood magic of dreaming and imagination will help you find balance in your current life.

CHAPTER 2

LAUNCHING PAD: JUGGLING ACT

66 ———————————————————

*"Learn early that perfection is impossible and
not something to aspire to as it is unreachable."*

——————————————————— 99

From 1995 to 2005, chaos, caffeine, and carpools were my life. Newborns, bottles, diapers, toys, toddlers, and tantrums defined these years. Andrew, my "old soul" and precocious son, was born in 1995. Jacob, my sensitive, calm, observant, and more introverted middle child, was born in 1998, and Ashley, my girly, kind, and outgoing daughter, was born in 2001. This decade was an adventure filled with joy, pandemonium, and craziness. I truly loved staying at home with my three kids. They were joyful and handfuls all at once. With three kids under five at one point, life moved quickly, with barely time to catch my breath. The highs and lows of navigating my career, trying cases, arguing in an appellate court, and wearing suits were swapped for the complexities of playgroup schedules, gymnastic classes, mommy and me song groups, temper tantrum solutions, and nap schedules. The job of mommy replaced my yearning for a big career. I did not see myself going to trial on significant cases anymore, and I rocked the job of mom.

A two-year-old, a four-year-old. and a seven-year-old ran my life. I was frazzled, dazed, and tired while I ran from Little League games to dance classes, carpools, and then home for naps. My life was filled with birthday parties, sticky fingers, and toys strewn across the basement floor. These years were defined by moments, not months. I would not trade those days, and I desperately miss them now. The statement that the years are short and the days are long is so true. Trying to "kill the day" during inclement weather when we had nothing to do on a sleepy and snow-strewn Saturday was painful. Hours spent on the basement floor helping my kids build complex zoos and pirate worlds with Playmobil® toys defined these early days. Tea parties with American Girl Dolls and art projects took the place of trials and brief writing that had previously defined my life as a lawyer.

There were times that I yearned for my old life back and missed the exhilaration I felt trying cases and helping clients. It now feels fleeting, and I would give anything to go back and fiercely hug those cranky kids in our large, bright, chaotic kitchen. Closing my eyes, I can smell cookies baking in the oven, I can see Jacob sitting on the kitchen floor putting together a complex puzzle, I can visualize Andrew doing homework at the computer in the office, and Ashley playing with her Barbies in her room. I blinked, and it all changed. My ex-husband left his successful law firm, and together, we launched a unique business in a nonexistent industry with no financial backing and no money for the startup. He left with nothing but an idea of a business, and I supported him.

I knew the reason I went to law school was to support myself or my family if anything shook up our lives. This decision was life-altering. The backup plan that I had envisioned in college now became our reality. We went from a very steady, easy life with defined traditional roles into the unknown abyss of a start-up venture. I was catapulted back into the work world.

My stay-at-home mom life came crashing down, and I dusted off my business suits and high heels to interview with law firms in Chicago. Instead of articulating my passion for law, I pitched this new business venture and concept. The business was a legal finance company where we would provide money to clients injured in car and work accidents. Lawyers are barred from giving money to their clients. When I was a workers' compensation lawyer, I spent many hours a day calling my clients' landlords and begging bill collectors to wait for my clients' cases to settle to collect from them. We had no options. Legal finance was going to level the playing field for injured clients with personal injury cases. I knew this service would be game-changing. I decided to go back to work for our new company and invest in myself for the benefit of my family instead of working for a law firm.

So it began. I started a business in an industry that was nonexistent for a service that every lawyer I met with told me would never work. In fact, they emphatically proclaimed they would never refer their injured clients for this service and predicted the business would fail. Yes, that is correct. Legal funding, litigation finance, lawsuit loans, advance funding, and plaintiff funding are now an established industry. However, in 2004, it was an unknown service that lawyers would not even consider. When I approached lawyers about the business and asked them to refer their clients to our company, Oasis Financial, the lawyers laughed me out of their offices. The more people told me no, the harder I worked. I believed this service was a lifeline for people who worked paycheck to paycheck. I saw incredible value in assisting these clients with financial resources while they waited for their cases to settle or go to trial.

The next decade consisted of launching, marketing, and running Oasis Financial, a complex specialty finance business that started as just an idea and grew to a revenue of $70 million with over 150 employees, including a large call center, when we exited in 2013. I hired, trained, and managed the inside and outside sales teams and ran the law firm marketing for this business. Nurturing a business to help it grow from a start-up to a well-oiled machine is grueling work. The struggle is real. Starting your own business is not for everyone and not for the faint-hearted. It will drain your energy and push you to limits you had no idea existed.

I experienced various challenges during this period of life. My biggest takeaways were about juggling my young family with a startup venture. Dealing with all of this while having sleepless nights working on the business brand and simultaneously raising three precocious and rambunctious kids was a circus. The most important aspect of my life was parenting my three children. However, I would not let the business fail, as we needed this to work to pay the mortgage and to support our family. My kids would not miss out on anything because of this new business. I had focus, drive, and abounding energy. Failure was not an option.

Over the next decade, I developed, managed, and nurtured a sales and marketing team that successfully created the foundation for the most well-known legal finance brand in the country. I attended conferences across the country and began the journey of meeting clients who would eventually help me launch my new business. I did all this while driving carpools, working for charitable organizations, and cooking dinners for the family. At that time, I had some balance as I was working from home two days a week and going to the office two to three days per week. Little did I know, but this business set the foundation for my future endeavors and for this book.

For working mothers of young children, is balance even possible? Having the right strategy for your work-life balance is imperative. With very few role models, I had to figure out how to find help for my children, how to multitask, and how to prioritize. It is crucial to realize you cannot manage work and family alone. Your spouse should be your biggest cheerleader and teammate during this period. You should form a vision of how you will work together to raise your children and multitask at home. Have weekly meetings with your spouse in order to ensure you both have time for work, for yourselves, and for your marriage. Many couples in their early 30s make their kids the center of their world. Although putting the children first like we did is admirable, it often leads to cracks in the foundation of your marriage. Make sure to block time for date nights and alone time. Communication with your spouse is the key to a healthy life.

Find help for your home and your family. My children look back at the Oasis years and label this decade the years of the revolving nannies. We did not have many family members nearby who could help us full-time, and I had to rely on au pairs and hired help to fill in the gaps and help me with my kids' busy schedules. Travel, soccer, competitive dance teams, tennis, hockey, baseball, and student council… the list was endless, and I barely had time to think. I was fortunate to have my sister, Jennifer, close by to help us sometimes, and a best friend, Nina, who pitched in with rides home from school and helped with homework. One very successful mother and law firm owner I know proudly tells people that she has a team of helpers in her home who assist with running her busy family and household. She says that she feels like she has to explain having this help to others, as they can be judgmental. Do not feel guilty if you can afford this help.

Finding good child care is crucial. Spend the extra money to make sure that your kids have proper afterschool programs, babysitters, and responsible help in your home. Ask your friends and family for guidance and assistance as well. Surround yourself with friends and family and ask for help when things are difficult. Clear communication with the people you care about is crucial. Many women (including me) try to show the world that they can do it all. Asking for help is not a sign of weakness. Vulnerability is important at this stage of life. Exhaustion and burnout can derail you. Knowing when you are feeling tired and overwhelmed will prevent a breakdown later on. Also, do not hold yourself to too high of a standard. Perfection is not the goal.

Asking for help is not a sign of weakness.

During this time, I was a perfectionist. I failed to set proper boundaries. No was not a word in my vocabulary. I found myself saying yes to many projects. I was the class mom at the children's schools, on the board of Children's Memorial Hospital, entertained for every holiday at our home, and hosted a constant parade of the kids' friends at our house. I also said yes when my friends asked me for plans or for favors. I did not understand the word no. I was on autopilot and did not have the self-awareness and knowledge to set boundaries. It is imperative that you set clear boundaries and make "no" a go-to word in your vocabulary. You cannot and should not be everything to everyone; perfection should not be the goal. Why is it so difficult for many women to say no when asked for a favor? Once you set boundaries and articulate your hard stops to people, it will become easier to set your boundaries. Prioritize important tasks and people who mean a lot to you, and politely reject the people and situations that overwhelm you.

Learn early that perfectionism is impossible and not something to aspire to, as it is unreachable. Psychologist Dr. Michaela Dunbar's book *You've Got This: Seven Steps to a Life You Love*[2] explains how to be "perfectly imperfect." She encourages her readers to "get to a point where you can accept that not everything in life will go perfectly." Her book helps you learn mindfulness, which is a practice where you can sit in the world, detaching from "unhelpful thoughts," and trains you to see

---

[2] Dunbar, Michaela. *You've Got This: Seven Steps to a Life You Love*, HarperCollins, 2023

the world through an objective lens. Dr. Dunbar provides templates for the practice of saying *no*. She explains that the reason people ask you for everything is because they know you can do a good job. She states that after saying no, you should show "gratitude, but also be very clear around the fact that you can't do it." Furthermore, she says not to apologize or explain. "There's no need to over-explain because that reinforces the idea to yourself that simply asserting boundaries and needs isn't good enough."

Another way to help regulate yourself when you crave balance and calm in the midst of a turbulent period is to work on yourself with "emotional regulation." Learn what your triggers are, and hire a coach. If you can work on managing your emotions in stressful situations, you can function at a very high level, according to Kellerman and Seligman in their book *Tomorrowmind*.[3] In fact, the most "mature leaders and professionals who operate at the highest levels are blunt communicators" and do not "just react." Hiring a coach can help you succeed at anything you set your mind to. Many people seek business coaches at work or hire therapists when they are on the verge of mental and physical burnout. I encourage you to do what I failed to do. I did not realize the burnout path I was on and did not seek emotional or professional coaching until much later in life when I was already struggling. If you can set this coaching up preventatively, you will avoid the struggles and mistakes made when you are on the edge of a breakdown.

---

[3] Seligman, Martin E. P., and Gabriella Rosen Kellerman. *Tomorrowmind Martin E. P. Seligman*, Atria Books, 2023

Hiring a coach can help you succeed at anything you set your mind to.

Coaching comes in all different forms. You can hire an executive coach, a health coach, or a therapist. Once you are in touch with your emotions and can sit back and look at your life more objectively, you will assess the type of coaching you need. If your budget is an issue, make this a goal and a priority. You can also read self-help books (which you are doing right now), listen to podcasts, attend virtual events and mastermind conferences where other women share their stories, and professionals work with groups to cover topical issues.

Another strategy is to form a group of other working moms who can support you. Former COO of Facebook (now Meta) Sheryl Sandberg addresses the idea of women supporting other working women in her book *Lean In: Women, Work, and the Will to Lead*.[4] Sandberg offers valuable insights and strategies that can help women who feel isolated; she offers advice to balance work and family. Here are some ways in which *Lean In* can support and empower women facing these challenges:

- Sandberg advocates for women to build support networks and *Lean In* circles to support their colleagues through challenges they face at work and home.

---

[4] Sandberg, Sheryl. *Lean In: Women, Work, and the Will to Lead*, Random House, 2015

- She helps redefine work and family issues for women by helping them set realistic goals based on their values.

- She equips women with self-advocacy skills to work on boundaries and communication. Her advice allowed me to advocate for myself to get a raise at work and to negotiate with an all-male-dominated board of directors effectively who tried to bully me into accepting a lower salary than the men at my company.

- She also addresses the issue of mom guilt. (My advice…Let it go!)

Sandberg's background working as an executive for Google and then Facebook allowed her to cultivate her theories in male-dominated industries. She watched women in these companies who held themselves back from leadership roles due to societal limitations and expectations and created her book to empower women so they could meet their full potential. Sandberg's book inspired me to name my first company Lean In, as we were a female-owned finance company doing business as Momentum Funding. However, the operating company was named for this groundbreaking book and the power it gave me to achieve success in a male-dominated industry. This book will help you advocate for career advancement and will also show you how to build strong bonds with women in your network.

---

*…finding balance is about flexibility
and forgiveness.*

While climbing the corporate ladder it is important to add balance to your life by blocking time to unwind. You work hard, and you deserve to have a break. On the days you have help, make sure to do things for yourself. Take a break by enjoying a spa day, lunch with a friend, or shopping. Communicate with your family, your employers, and work colleagues to make sure that they all know when you are feeling burned out. Everyone feels overwhelmed at times, and finding balance is about flexibility and forgiveness. You are not a failure if you let things go. Your success rides on the days that you find the balance and on you letting go of the perception that perfection is the goal. Do not discount spontaneity and fun, as they are the antidote to perfectionism and rigidity.

Managing your time is another key to your success. Your calendar is your best friend. I have always adhered to block time scheduling. I now use an Outlook calendar that syncs with Google, and I add all tasks and meetings to this calendar. An example of this is blocking time for team meetings and emails and even blocking time for thinking. During this quiet time, carve out time to just be. Stay off devices, clear your head, and head to a park or beach with a good book. For me, using uninterrupted blocks of time to decompress allows me to focus and clear my head. Also, before I go to sleep, I make a comprehensive to-do list that allows me to take all the unfinished business of the day and put it down so that I can check items off my list the next day.

Having fun on the run is another strategy that I found helpful during these chaotic years of juggling work and family. Know when you have reached your limit and then push through and change the trajectory of your day. Some days, it is hard to get out of bed. On one of those days, I woke up, made lunches for the kids, and packed my workout bag with clothing to wear for a business meeting. The morning also consisted of meal prepping for the family dinner. I left the house at 6:00 a.m. and went to the gym for my workout. Midway through the rigorous workout, I felt like I couldn't make it. In fact, I felt as if an elephant was sitting on my chest. If I could have simply gone home and climbed back into my comfy bed and pulled the covers over my head, this would have been the day for that. Do you have days when you don't think you can go on? Life is not what it looks like on Facebook or in the movies. Nope. It is messy and hard and complicated and blurry, and there are days when everything looks gray and blah, and work seems insurmountable.

You have the power to make anything in your life happen.

On the days when everything seems overwhelming, push through it. I did this on that day when I wanted to crawl back under the covers. I pushed myself during the workout when I wanted to quit. I pushed myself during the workday that I wanted to skip. I pushed myself to go to the gym, where I had the most incredible workout, and then killed it at work. I ordered pizza for my staff. Yep, greasy, gooey, sausage and onion pizza, and then I ordered wine, beer, and champagne, and we just had *fun*. Yes, fun at work. We FaceTimed our clients and told them to pop bottles of champagne and partake in the bubbly with us. They did it! This then turned into a fun event. We labeled it "FaceTime Friday with a Law Firm," and the clients loved this ritual. No one else is show-ing up to push you. You have to be your own cheerleader. Self-advocacy and motivation need to come from within. You have the power to make anything in your life happen.

All the creative juices flow when things are the most overwhelm-ing, messy, crazy, and just plain hard! You cannot appreciate good days if you do not know what it feels like to have a bad day. On the days when you are overwhelmed, go home, fill the bathtub, light a candle, pour yourself a glass of wine, and soak. Find a magazine or good book and read it while soaking in the tub. Put on your favorite relaxing playlist and push through it all because you turned your challenging day into a success story. Tomorrow is a new day.

Set goals for your day that highlight how you focus on your mind-set and attitude to succeed. These goals can include personal affirmations about positivity and resilience. Manifesting is the notion that you can set a goal or a positive mindset and then make whatever you want happen. I have a "success-only" mindset, and I am also a risk-taker in business and life. I surround myself with the kind of people and environment that will help me foster a "success-only" mindset. It does take a village to raise a family. I highly recommend that you define your village early on. Learn who to lean on and collaborate with to create a village of support to carpool, take each other's kids when one of you needs help, and meet for happy hours and themed parties frequently. All work and no play will lead to burnout and a lack of balance in your life. Balance is the key to success.

Top 5 Ways to Avoid Burnout:

1. Prioritize important aspects of your life.
2. Hire help if needed and as soon as you can afford it.
3. Take frequent breaks and take time out for yourself and self-care.
4. Carve out time to be still.
5. Do not feel guilty.

CHAPTER 3

MOMENTUM: SEASONS OF CHANGE

66 ——————————————————

"Sometimes, when everything is falling apart, it is all really coming together."

—————————————————— **99**

After leaving Oasis, we decided to start another financial service business. To launch this new business, we met with investors, private equity groups, and hedge funds to raise the capital needed to start the new company. I put on my business suit and attended a women's networking event at a bank in downtown Chicago. The moderators asked each group to present their innovative business ideas and financial requests to a panel of Northwestern University business school professors. The first group stood up and said they were seeking $100,000 in *Shark Tank* fashion to start a nouveau bridal boutique. The next group requested $200,000 for a unique fashion jewelry business. I was last and said, "I am seeking $40 million to start a legal finance business." The room went silent. After that pitch, one of the professors took my contact information and introduced me to a prominent angel investor who became our mentor and assisted in the search for financing. He set up meetings for us where we pitched our idea for Momentum Funding to hedge funds and private equity groups. In a short time frame, we raised $40 million to start the business, Momentum Funding. I was a co-founder and president of this company. Within four years, the business progressed from an idea to a multi-million dollar company with revenue of over $30 million, and we sold the business in 2019.

The quick success trajectory of Momentum Funding did not come without a heavy cost. The more successful the business became, the harder it was to balance my family and home life. Let's focus on the positive mindset and what it takes to make a business prosper while still protecting your peace. By looking back at what did and did not work for me, I can help you with your path to success as you learn to balance work with your home life. If you can learn to recognize where there are fractures in your life and learn how to avoid resentment, you can make changes that allow you to create the space needed to succeed with career and family.

While building and scaling Momentum Funding, I traveled at least ten days per month to visit clients, met with law firms in over 20 states, spoke in hundreds of law firms and at events, and attended numerous conferences nationwide throughout the years. The frenetic pace of building this business caused significant stress. As an entrepreneur, you touch every part of a business. As a business owner you manage all departments of the company. Marketing, technology, sales, finance, and the eventual sale of the company dominated a significant portion of my time and energy. I had many sleepless nights and worked seven days a week. Building a brand and a business in a short four-year time frame from inception to sale took the wind out of me. This treacherous path to success and achievement destroyed my marriage and affected my family. The most difficult part of this business was that we had to move our family across the country.

The business's success relied on us living closer to our clients, who were primarily concentrated in the Southeast. My children had to move out of their childhood home to relocate, attend new schools, and meet new friends. The guilt I felt for encouraging this move and for the difficulties they suffered because of it plagued me. However, true growth often comes from hardships. When I look back and remember that journey and the building of that business, I now see clearly what I did well and where I could make improvements. I did not have the calm and balance that was needed for my personal life to excel. The more my life was falling apart, the more successful the business became. The intensity I injected into the business depleted me.

True growth often comes from taking risks and admitting failures. If things come too easy, you cannot appreciate when things are truly good.

As my professional brand and business grew and blossomed, my home life fell apart. However, sometimes, when everything is falling apart, it is all really coming together. This difficult time in my life prepared me for the next chapter. Although the Momentum period was challenging, the habits I formed and the lessons I learned about building a team were invaluable. True growth often comes from taking risks and admitting failures. If things come too easy, you cannot appreciate when things are truly good.

Resilience is often built through intense struggle.

Resilience is often built through intense struggle. Because of the challenges they have witnessed, my children have become adaptable, outgoing, and strong in business and life. They watched me multitask and juggle work and family, and they learned how to push through difficulties to achieve their own resilience and success. Now that they are all working, they understand that sacrifice and hard work are the foundation for prosperity. During the Momentum Funding years, I became a master at the tools a working mother needs to work hard and be efficient.

What are the lessons I have learned along the way that I can share with you? How can you attempt to stay grounded and focused when the world around you spirals out of control? Forming healthy habits and surrounding yourself with the right people will help you immeasurably. Where do you start? Start now. Start small. Start simply. Habits cannot be changed all at once. Habits are changed one small step at a time. I did not wake up one day saying, "I am going to meditate daily, eat healthy, take breaks, and set boundaries." I started with one thing at a time. I ordered a meditation cushion and placed it near a window overlooking the preserve and lake in my backyard. I sat on the cushion when I felt stressed. Soon, this became a habit, and I started going to this meditative corner every morning. I started drinking a glass of water daily with my vitamins and ordered ingredients for a smoothie that enhances health and boosts energy. I set an alarm on my phone that reminds me to stand up and take a break every hour. I signed up for workout classes and made them a weekly routine.

One book that helped me form productive routines is *Atomic Habits: An Easy & Proven Way to Build Good Habits & Break Bad Ones* by James Clear.[5] The author presents a framework for creating impactful habits and teaches that small changes can yield major results. This book provides the toolbox to reshape your thinking in order to change and develop habits that will improve your life. One invaluable lesson I took away from *Atomic Habits* is to associate difficult habits with a renewed mindset. Instead of saying, "I *have* to wake up early and make breakfast for my family," change the word "have" to the word "get" and state, "I *get* to wake up early and make breakfast for my family." Rephrasing how you interpret the world and recognizing daily blessings in everyday moments changes your mindset. I am blessed that I get to live a fulfilling life surrounded by family and friends. I add new healthy habits each month and build on these routines to live an authentic life.

Personal Habits

Currently, I focus on my morning routine. When I was juggling the kids and Momentum Funding, I was usually rushed in the mornings. I now wake up early, and my morning habits create a starting

---

[5] Clear, James. *Atomic Habits: Tiny Changes, Remarkable Results: An Easy & Proven Way to Build Good Habits & Break Bad Ones*, Penguin Random House, 2018

point for a productive and positive day. My best days start by waking up, making strong coffee, and slow dancing with my husband in our kitchen to one of our favorite country songs. After he leaves for work, I call my best friend Michelle from my cozy office. At least five mornings a week, we laugh and cry together. These daily calls launch my day by adding joy and laughter. We have helped each other through many difficult and trying times. Hearing her voice makes me smile and reassures me when I have doubts. We tell each other everything; we share our inner fears and stressors. Since we have such an innate long-term understanding of each other's personalities and triggers, we know just the right way to advise, calm, and center each other. From college to midlife, Michelle and I have raised five children, gone through two divorces, reinvented our careers, and enjoyed forty years of laughter and tears.

Having that strong lifeline helps so much. Despair arises when you have no one on the other end of the phone line. When you have that person who knows all sides of you and who supports you by listening, you can go through the peaks and valleys of your life. The tides will turn. Life will throw a lot at you. Find a friend who will always tell you the cold, hard truth, even when it is difficult to handle. I am incredibly fortunate to have several close friends to confide in and share all of life's trials and tribulations with. I am also fortunate to have my sister, Jennifer, who is close in age with me and a sounding board for life's constant stressors. If you are lucky enough to have more than one special friend, you are truly blessed. It is better to have a few close friendships than many acquaintances.

Other important habits are to foster a positive mindset and to try to stay focused on the present. How can you stay present? James Clear's book provides a way to transform "frustration into delight." Mindset changes can be changed by fixing the habits and "motivation rituals" associated with various behaviors. For example, if you want to feel happier, discover what makes you truly happy and form a routine around that act or routine every time before you do what you love. An example of something you love is a bubble bath or petting your dog. Clear gives an example: "Maybe you take three deep breaths and smile. Three deep breaths. Smile. Take the bath. Repeat. Eventually, you'll begin to associate this breathe-and-smile routine with being in a good mood." I practice using Clear's method to distract myself from negative thought patterns. When stressful situations arise, I now have this healthy habit to lean on.

Your attitude will determine how you process gratitude.

I do not spend too much time thinking negatively. Attitude is everything. I have the skills to shift my mindset with deep breaths and mantras. At the end of this book, I list my affirmations. Make your own list and incorporate it into your life so you can live with gratitude. Your attitude will determine how you process gratitude. In addition to listing affirmations, make a daily gratitude list. Start each day by reading these gratitude lists and affirmations and end the day by reviewing them; add to your lists regularly. I keep Oprah Winfrey's book *What I Know for*

Sure[6] on my nightstand. The beautiful book is a compilation of essays that highlight the significance of gratitude in your life. Her practice of gratitude has contributed to her success. She states, "Be thankful for what you have; you'll end up having more. If you concentrate on what you don't have, you will never, ever have enough." Oprah states that "we get so focused on the difficulty of our climb that we lose sight of simply having a mountain to climb." She acknowledges that being in a constant state of gratitude is difficult and not easy. When you feel least thankful is when you are in most need of gratitude to give you perspective. Oprah's focus on being grateful is a constant reminder to keep moving forward and to find joy and possibility in the simplest of moments. It is not always easy to stay grateful; there will be days when you lose momentum, and negativity can seep in. Recalibrate your thinking, and you can change the energy. For me, having Oprah's book at my bedside is a constant reminder to stay positive.

In addition to these lists, other daily habits help me stay grounded, happy, and focused. After my morning routine of dancing, my phone call, and having my smoothie, I meditate. The designated meditation station in my home office is the setting for perfect mornings. I play meditations on my phone using an app called Buddhify. These meditations meet me where I am—feeling stressed, waking up, work, break, etc. Keeping yourself accountable also relates to your home life and health. Come up with your own morning or evening routine. Rising before your kids are awake will give you some personal time to focus

---

[6] Winfrey, Oprah. *What I Know For Sure*. Macmillan, 2014

on yourself. If you are not a morning person, you can have an evening ritual like a warm bath accompanied by a good book.

Your most important healthy habit should be some form of physical fitness or workout. Many women claim they are too busy to work out. However, meeting many successful doctors, lawyers, and CEOs, I have learned that the most successful people find time to incorporate exercise into their daily routine. My workouts consist of a variety of activities. Finding a workout that you enjoy and can physically tolerate will depend on your age, fitness level, and health. I do a Monday Tabata class, a Tuesday Barre class, weight train several times per week, and play pickleball as much as possible.

Finding a role model for your fitness routines will help empower and motivate you to meet your fitness goals. Recently, I partnered with Maureen White, a fitness instructor who has abounding energy and juggles her career effectively with parenting her two young children. She states, "No one can transform you. Transformation cannot begin until you have looked within yourself and taken responsibility for your actions and choices. Then you must commit to making the necessary changes and be willing to work hard for them. Only then can true transformation begin." It is never too late to start a health and fitness routine. Habits can be formed at any stage or age. Make it a priority to keep your fitness routine a part of your daily life.

Another influence for me who has helped me form healthy habits is Dr. Jen Ashton. I follow Dr. Ashton on her weekly email blasts, *Today's Ajenda*. She states, "I believe every woman, of every age, who physically can, should lift weights."[7] She discusses a theory called NEAT, which stands for Non-Exercise Activity Thermogenesis, and explains that studies "have shown that shorter spurts of exercise… can be just as good as one longer workout." By making changes in your lifestyle and adding more movement into your daily work day, you can improve your overall health. One tip I use during the workday is to do what I call "work and walk." I put my headphones on and make a call while walking around the block. I keep weights in my office and set timers. Every hour, I take a break and use the weights to target a specific body part. If you are in an office setting, take frequent breaks throughout the day and have a meeting on a walk with a work colleague. Also, I have recently started playing pickleball, which is a great way to get your heart rate up and have some social interaction at the same time.

Self-care is imperative in order to keep from burning out. Mothers often feel guilty after long days at work. They do not feel that they can treat themselves to a spa treatment or dinner out with a friend because they don't see their kids during the day. The guilt needs to go. Take a trip with friends, go out with your book club, and make that spa appointment. Your husband and children will be happy when you are happy. Then, when you feel you are about to burn out, take a break and practice self-care. Book a manicure or a massage and find a way to unwind and relax. If you cannot afford treatments, do an at-home spa event and turn your home into an oasis. Amazon has all kinds of reasonably priced spa accessories, such as pedicure bowls, bath bombs, lotions, and massagers. Spending time with friends, vacationing and

---

[7] "Today's Ajenda," accessed 2024, https://todays-ajenda.beehiiv.com/p/todays-ajenda-issue-9.

date nights with your spouse, and exercising regularly are all imperative for you to be 100 percent at home and at work. Know that wherever you are in your journey, you can always reset.

Your husband and children will be happy when you are happy.

Boundary setting and putting your phone away at meals and after dinner will help create rituals of connection with your spouse and children. Remember, the kids are watching you. If you cannot be present during mealtimes and transitions and are only giving your family partial attention because your phone is demanding your time, they will learn from your distracted behaviors. When you make a mistake, laugh at yourself; never take yourself too seriously. Seeking professional help for your mental health is not an admission of failure. Therapy is an incredibly healthy strategy to help you form self-awareness and recognize your triggers. A good therapist helps you set boundaries and form habits you need for a "success-only" mindset.

Boundary setting and putting your phone away at meals and after dinner will help create rituals of connection with your spouse and children.

Music is also a great way to disconnect from the busyness of life. Music can calm the mind and enhance cognition. My favorite quote about music is from U2 singer Bono, who said, "Music can change the world because it can change people." The Mozart Effect is a widely recognized theory about how Mozart's music calms people down and boosts their cognitive abilities. A study in *Health Psychology Review*[8] showed that music lowered people's cortisol levels and deduced that music directly reduces stress responses and promotes relaxation. So why not make a playlist with your favorite songs and listen to them while driving and when you take your digital detox? Have your playlists playing softly in the background while you work. Good music can be the backdrop for your life. Hearing certain songs transports me back to time periods and brings out the emotions I felt at those times. Music can definitely trigger memories and regulate your mood.

On the other hand, when you take a walk, it is often a good idea to walk in silence to enjoy nature. When you are constantly inundated with chaos, a quiet walk in the woods or in nature can help reset your equilibrium. Having a pet will allow you to disengage while working if you are working from home. During COVID, I decided to get a dog. This was a great way for me to have forced breaks and kept me moving. I worked with her at my side, and she kept me active. Also, she was a calming force when I had stressful events at work. She constantly reminds me to be in the present.

Charitable endeavors will also help feed your soul. Most companies encourage their employees to get involved with charitable endeavors in their communities. You may wonder how I can even think

---

[8] de Witte, M., Pinho, A. da S., Stams, G. J., Moonen, X., Bos, A. E. R., & van Hooren, S. (2020). Music therapy for stress reduction: a systematic review and meta-analysis. *Health Psychology Review*, *16*(1), 134–159. https://doi.org/10.1080/17437199.2020.1846580

to advise you that finding a charity you are passionate about would be something you can fit into your already hectic schedule. However, you can engage your friends and family in charitable projects. If you find a cause you are passionate about and believe in, I promise it will energize you in countless ways. Find hands-on activities that will engage your family and friends, and you will feel calm and at peace. When my daughter, Ashley, was about thirteen, she lived in a typical teenage bubble in an affluent suburb, surrounded by excess and materialism and disconnected from the world. One day while watching the news, I saw that a devastating tornado had wiped out the town of Moore, Oklahoma. Seeing the overwhelming devastation, I realized the juxtaposition of my daughter's privileged life and this community that had lost everything. We traveled to Oklahoma to perform disaster relief. Sifting through the debris at a trailer park decimated by the vicious storm, we found nothing left but pieces of photos. Entire families' lives had been torn to shreds in a matter of seconds. We assisted at Goodwill, helped homeowners find their possessions, and fed families who lacked power. These memories have stayed with us for a decade.

Professional Habits

Along with forming personal habits, I created many professional habits that nurtured Momentum Funding to grow and thrive. To start a successful business, you must engage in business rhythms and habits that keep you and your team accountable. Start with one habit a week and add additional habits. Morning huddles are a great way to start the day. End-of-week success and challenge meetings wrap up the week with "Focus Fridays." As a team leader, do not underestimate the value of in-person communication and meetings. I hosted frequent team re-treats out of town for my sales and marketing teams at both Oasis and Momentum. Employees will open up when you take them out of the work environment. You will learn more about your team and your company during a three-day company retreat than you would during months of in-office meetings.

Building personal relationships with work colleagues will help your business by fostering a culture of loyalty and commitment. We live in a time when we have turned in-person communities into online communities. What happened to villages and in-person work environ-ments? Chat rooms, social media communities, and Zoom meetings have replaced them. What will the future hold for this disconnected way of life? How can society overcome the lack of human connection that online digitization has replaced? Texts and Slack channels at work have replaced phone calls. When people work in offices now, they do not even walk over to their managers to ask questions. Instead, they use Slack, text, or email. Eye contact and human interaction are at risk of becoming the exception. The habit of showing up in person is key. As a business owner or leader, breaking the cycle of impersonal commu-nication will set you apart and build a company based on trust.

Many women in the work world have expressed that the new way of working remotely has left them lonely and devoid of energy. How can you combat this loneliness and isolation while building your busi-ness and managing your family? Some strategies that will help include prioritizing what is important and setting realistic expectations and goals. Make sure you do not compare yourself to others and do not spend too much time on social media. Create robust support systems and communicate with your spouse, friends, and family over the phone. Ask for help and share your frustrations and your wins with those around you. Find routines and ways of connecting with friends on a regular basis. Form a group that shares common interests with you. I have always had a book club. This group of strong women helps ground me, provides a group of friends as a sounding board, and pushes me to escape during busy weeks with a good book that transports me to another world. Time management is also necessary; tools that you can use for time management are prolific. There are apps for calendars and productivity that make it easy to stay organized.

Delegation is everything and imperative for success. Say no often. Practice this word daily. Recently, I spent time with Jenn Gore Cuthbert, a beautiful, brilliant trial lawyer, law firm owner, social media influencer, and mother of three children under 12. I asked her what her secret was, and she quickly replied, "I have a lot of help! I have an entire team at work and at home to help me get through the work week. I have a nanny, a chef, and an executive assistant." Good for her. She gets it. She has delegated tasks so she can be present for her kids and her work. She did not start out like that. When she started her business, she had limited funds and little or no help. You can easily start out by hiring a young helper or neighbor and work up to more help. You want your time with your family to be quality time. If you are exhausted from working at home and at the office, you will not be fully present and at your best with your family.

Decorate your space to create your own Zen Zone to help you relax and focus. My office has soothing colors of light pinks and grays. I have a whiteboard with my affirmations pinned on it. Keep your gratitude list and affirmations close at all times. Many women now work from home and have to create home offices or corners of their homes for their new remote environments. Although during COVID, it seemed optimal when this work-from-home movement first occurred, over time, many women have expressed how isolating and depressing this model truly is. Mental health can be significantly impacted by it. A Pew Research Center study found that women had high levels of psychological stress during the pandemic.[9] The World Health Organization reported a 25 percent increase in anxiety and depression and highlighted that women and young people experienced more severe impacts than other groups. Not having a friend to walk down to the corner coffee shop with during a break or someone to chat with at the water cooler has fostered an isolation culture that needs to be understood.

What you look at daily will also inspire you to be successful. The expression that I have worked and lived by is: **Make it happen**. I have journals and signs around me while I work that state that phrase and another sign on my desk that says, "Life is what you make it." If you surround yourself with décor that soothes and fills your soul with Zen, it will help you remain focused and keep your work flowing with purpose. Escape. Dream. Believe. **Make it Happen.**

---

[9] Gramlich, John. "Mental Health and the Pandemic: What U.S. Surveys Have Found," *Pew Research Center*, March 2, 2023

True happiness comes when tasks are accomplished, and you feel whole, present, and connected.

When you break from your habits, do not berate yourself. It is okay. You can fall down; you can rise up. You can and will do hard things. True happiness comes when tasks are accomplished and you feel whole, present, and connected. Once you are able to work on your mindset and create positive habits, it is important to work on your fears and anxieties. Fear of failure and generalized anxiety have seeped into our culture and created a world filled with stress and worry. Young women are plagued by anxiety, and many cannot stop thinking about what may happen in the future. Our phones, the 24/7 news cycle, fear-mongering, weather scares, fires, movie and school shootings, and more have created a society filled with fear, panic attacks, and anxiety. Using habits and a positive mindset to dispel these fears and worries is key. Forming habits and working on creating balance will allow you to settle into a more calm mindset. Instead of thinking about the worst thing that could happen, reframe your thinking to think about what the best thing that could happen is. Although I have always had a "glass-half-full" philosophy, I used to approach my life with the worst-case scenario theory.

After attending an outdoor mindfulness retreat, I realized that the way I was thinking was not healthy. At this retreat, we were asked to climb a large pole with a bungee cord on our backs. Once I got to the top of the pole, I had to stand up and jump hundreds of feet to the ground. My fear was off the charts. I was with my daughter and did not want her to see me fail. While climbing the pole, I kept thinking about the worst things that could happen. If I fell off the pole, the guide was trained to help me. I knew he had a medical kit with him, and he did this type of work every day. When the event ended, we sat and shared our fears and thoughts with the group. The guide was able to explain to me that my thought of "what is the worst thing that could happen" should be changed to "what is the best thing that could happen." With that renewed and recalibrated positive mindset, I reframed the way I handled difficult situations.

Fear of failure and the expectation of perfectionism go back to your childhood. Maybe you had a parent who withheld love and affection unless you performed at a certain level or a parent who could not self-regulate his own emotions. Learn from your childhood triggers and work on yourself by understanding where you are creating some of the same patterns your parents fostered. When you make mistakes, admit them. Let your children know that you are sorry and that you are not going to be perfect all the time. When you are able to stay in the present and be in the moment, when you put your devices and phone away, and when you do the work to form positive habits, the fear will subside, and you will succeed.

The only way you can find peace and stay calm
is when you stay in the present.

What I have learned is that you cannot and will never be able to predict or know what the future holds. The only way you can find peace and stay calm is when you stay in the present. Peace is in the present. You need to be present in the moment. Plan trips, arrange fun outings, find your passion in hobbies, read books, and just be in the moment. Another one of my mantras is: "Peace in the present. Mind over matter. Live for the moment. Get rid of the chatter." I came up with this phrase when I started Momentum Funding. Originally, the company was going to be a workout business like Orange Theory, and that phrase was going to be the company's tagline. Once Momentum became the brand for the legal finance company, I was able to pivot and build the business. Whenever I found myself looking back or trying to think about the future, I used the mantra that I had created to keep focused on the present. Make your own mantra, or use mine. It will enhance your life and help you as you set out on your journey.

In addition to working on forming effective habits, it is imperative to surround yourself with the right people. A business starts with people. If you have the right partners and employees in place, it will go far. A book that has helped me build my businesses is *Good to Great* by Jim Collins.[10] Collins emphasizes the importance of having the right people in the proper roles. He states, "Sustained great results depend upon building a culture full of self-disciplined people who take disciplined action." When I started Momentum Funding, I hired several young women who had the skill sets I needed to build the business.

Eventually, several of these employees felt they were the entire business, and these women started poisoning the culture by talking

---

[10] Collins, Jim. *Good to Great: Why Some Companies Make the Leap...And Others Don't,* Harper Business, 2001

negatively about others and about the executives to the rest of the team. If an employee does not believe in the leader or CEO's vision, the brand and company will suffer as a result. I spent a lot of time diffusing drama. The negativity and damage to the culture were detrimental to the new business. My personal life was affected since it took a considerable amount of my time and energy. This is where quick-to-fire, slow-to-hire comes into place. I quickly let the employees go, and our business became even more profitable after their departure. Loyalty is key; surrounding yourself with employees who you know and trust is crucial at the startup stage of a business. Use your intuition when it comes to people and follow your gut when it tells you that an employee is a cancer. Your inner voice will guide you to make the best decisions as you lead.

Surround yourself with people who are honest with you.

Surround yourself with people who are honest with you. You do not need "yes people." Build a team of partners and team members who are there for you when the chips are down and who can provide you with honest feedback about your choices and decisions. Remember to be a good listener when your team members or partners have feedback. The difference between a good company and a great company has to do with creating a culture of freedom and responsibility where you are not a "tyrannical disciplinarian."[11] Collins states that leadership is not just about vision. It is "equally about creating a climate where the truth

---

[11] Collins, *Good to Great*, 74.

is heard and the brutal facts confronted…The good-to-great leaders understood this distinction." Companies were more successful when they fostered a culture where people felt heard and comfortable expressing their opinions. Communication and relationship building with team members is imperative to foster a healthy culture.

We spend more time at work than we do at home, and a work team often becomes a family. At Oasis Financial and Momentum Funding, a large part of the success of the companies stemmed from the relationships that I built with my sales and marketing teams personally and professionally. I reflect and realize that I sometimes went too far in mothering many of the young women who worked for me. However, this investment in their personal well-being fostered an environment where they felt safe confiding in me. I mentored and trained these young professionals and have watched them grow over the years with both families and careers.

Culture is key. Set expectations for your team to work as hard as you do. When you articulate a success-only mindset and create a collaborative culture, the motivation of team members will be a significant deciding factor in whether a company succeeds or fails. By creating a company where team members feel invested in the business, supported by the team leaders and managers, and part of something bigger than themselves, employees' jobs become careers. When team members feel heard and seen, and when the managers invest time and truly listen to their team, true greatness can be achieved. In a great company, people can make mistakes and learn from them instead of assigning blame.[12]

[12] Collins, *Good to Great*, 78.

When the leader is present, taking responsibility alongside team members and learning from mistakes or poor decisions, the company benefits in the long run.

I tried to always be present for my team. I was not always fully present and occasionally had difficult days. However, being vulnerable with your work colleagues by admitting when you are having an off day will help build trust. Admit when you are struggling and articulate how you feel. I went through difficult personal struggles while building Momentum Funding; my husband at the time was my business partner. We sometimes disagreed about how we ran the business, and this conflict filtered into our home life. Sometimes our team members were caught in the middle of our disagreements. As I look back now, I understand that I needed to create better work-life boundaries. Although I believe in mentoring employees in order to bring out the best in them, it is also imperative to keep healthy boundaries to separate work and home life.

Another tactic to work with a team when you are feeling off is to log off. Logging off by digitally detoxing is necessary in our world, which is filled with constant red alerts, text messages, Slack messages, emails, Zoom calls, and phone calls. Take time each day to go for a walk, enjoy nature, meditate, put your phone down, journal, call a friend, and just *be*. The work, the calls, the texts, emails, and messages will all be waiting for you when you tune back in.

...if you want to live an authentic and connected life, surround yourself with people who will support you with truth, loyalty, respect, gratitude, and appreciation.

People you choose to surround yourself with are often a reflection of who you are. The question is, who should you surround yourself with? What kind of life do you want? The answer is that if you want to live an authentic and connected life, surround yourself with people who will support you with truth, loyalty, respect, gratitude, and appreciation. A business coach I worked with said to be "slow to hire and quick to fire." This one sentence has helped me make difficult decisions regarding toxic employees and good hires. When you realize that an employee is draining your energy and causing stress for other team members, let them go quickly. Once you give them feedback and warnings and toxic behaviors continue, make a quick decision and fire them.

True grit and authenticity are formed by developing real relationships and putting the relationship first.

I have stayed in touch with many former employees who left and went to competitive companies or launched their own businesses. I am so proud of them. These colleagues know that to me, work was just that—work. I valued the person more than the organization. I always put the person first. To my salespeople who were working moms, I told them that the kids and family should come first. After sacrificing so much of myself to create a successful business at the expense of my marriage, I learned the hard way that what matters in life is not getting ahead, not putting work first, and not advancing at the expense of others. True grit and authenticity are formed by developing real relationships and putting the relationship first. As a boss, you will always win when you put the person first.

Surround yourself with employees who bring out the best in you, who will be there when the chips fall, who have your back, and who will fight with you and for you. Believing in yourself and that you will succeed is not enough. It is important to surround yourself with smart individuals who have different skill sets from yours and to listen. The most important skill in life, business, and parenting is listening. All too many entrepreneurs fail when they think they know it all and when they do not stop to listen to what others tell them. Surrounding yourself with "yes" people will not help you achieve your goals. Instead, partner with smart, emotionally intelligent people who are not afraid to tell you the cold, hard truth and feel comfortable calling you out.

When I started all three companies, I ran into many obstacles. I started, stopped, pivoted, and then started over yet again. I fell down, I got back up, and I kept working. I was persistent until the dust settled, and I could see clearly. Often, when you are starting a business, you have a laser focus on the plan. Many times, that plan fails; it is often when everything disintegrates that clarity appears. There will always be failures and disappointments on your journey, either in life or when starting your own business. The leaders who endure and suffer adversity and then push through hardships and pivot to find other roads to get to the finish line are the people who get to the other side and find success. Nothing in life or business is easy, and I always say, "If it were that easy, everyone would do it." Most businesses fail in the first year. I am fortunate that I started three businesses that were all successful. My success resulted from forming effective habits, surrounding myself with good people, pivoting when necessary with several iterations and ideas, and pushing through the difficulties.

Top 5 Habits for a Balanced Life:

1. Morning rituals with gratitude lists and affirmations.
2. Mindset habits to focus on positivity.
3. Business rhythms to keep your team on track.
4. Self-care.
5. Boundaries at home and at work.

CHAPTER 4

ROAD WARRIOR: TURNING POINTS

66 —————————————————————

*"It is all in your attitude, and when you have
gratitude, your energy bounces off people and
can be infectious."*

————————————————————— **99**

Momentum's name came about when my son, Andrew, and I brainstormed ideas for a mind-body workout business. When we pivoted to start Momentum Funding as a legal finance business, we kept the name, as it connoted moving life forward with purpose. Ironically, the years we lived in Boca Raton, Florida, building Momentum, were years when I was not living my life with balance, self-awareness, truth, or purpose. Instead of life moving forward, I was stuck on a never-ending treadmill. I was incredibly unhappy and felt paralyzed. I had no passion for the business I built and did not have healthy habits in place; however, the business and life lessons I learned during this chapter of my life have given me perspective and expertise that I can now share with you. Frequent business travel nationwide resulted in the growth of a robust personal network, significant business relationships, and a strong personal brand. The productivity tools that I learned during these years helped the business excel. I will share the lessons I learned along the way related to travel, organization, mindset, and networking that led to the success of this company.

Business travel is an art. During the Momentum years, I traveled approximately 10-12 days per month. I left my busy family to visit clients, attend conferences, and present legal education seminars in law firms. At the height of my career, I was endlessly on the road, logging frequent flier miles and spending countless hours in airports across the country. When we raised millions of dollars in capital to start Momentum Funding, we explained to the investors that to be successful in our legal finance business, we would be road warriors and visit potential clients to encourage them to refer Momentum to the clients who needed financial help. As a result, I hit the road on a regular basis. Through this experience, I can now share many travel tricks with you.

You will have more luck with fewer canceled flights and delays if you fly out in the morning. The later in the day you fly, the greater the chances you will get delayed. My mantra is early flights make perfect nights. One day, I traveled to another city to make a 9:30 a.m. meeting. I had a two-hour block of time at the airport. I traveled in my workout clothes and went right to the gym in my destination city. I had a quick workout and shower at the health club to prepare for my meeting. Joining a health club that has locations in many cities is beneficial for this reason. However, you can also use workout apps like Mindbody, which allow you to book yoga and other fitness classes in any city across the United States.

Use your time in the air to dream and create. This book was born on a long flight. In fact, my most creative and productive moments have occurred on airplanes. Shutting out the world and using a meditation app to help you relax and tune into the right mindset is crucial. Unless you are facing a deadline, do not plan on doing traditional work on the plane. Let your mind wander and see where it takes you. In the air, no one can call or interrupt you. This calming time can bring transformation. My most innovative entrepreneurial ideas and brainstorming sessions have happened up in the air. I am the most creative when I fly. Block out your Wi-Fi so you will not be interrupted during this Zen Zone time.

Mindset is everything when traveling; inevitably, when you travel frequently, you will have delays. It is best to keep a positive attitude of gratitude. When faced with challenges, this positivity can be infectious. On a cold, gray, dreary day, a sleet and snowstorm delayed my flight out of St. Louis. It was the last flight out, with a layover in Atlanta before my flight back to Fort Lauderdale. Things did not look good for me to make my connection. I desperately missed my kids. I had an epiphany; if we could board the plane more efficiently and more quickly, there was a better chance I could make my Atlanta connection. I approached the gate attendant, who was responsible for informing the St. Louis passengers we would probably not make our Atlanta connections that evening. He calmly informed me it was unlikely we would make it home that night. I looked at the time we were scheduled to arrive and realized that if we could board the flight ten minutes quicker, I would probably make my connection to Ft. Lauderdale. I looked around the boarding terminal at all the annoyed passengers. "Sir, would you mind if I helped you with the boarding process?" I asked.

"Lady," he said with an exasperated sigh. "Look around this place. Anything you can do will be appreciated. But it is highly unlikely you can move these people any quicker." And with that, he handed me the microphone he was using to advise the passengers. I took a deep breath and shouted out, "Ladies and gentlemen, who would like to get home tonight to make your connections?" The depleted and exhausted passengers bundled up in their heavy coats with their cumbersome, bulky luggage barely even looked up at me. I changed my tone and stood in front of the desk. "I don't think you heard me, St. Louis!" I belted out. "How many of you want to get home tonight? I have a family waiting for me and desperately want to make my Atlanta connection. If you all cooperate to expedite the boarding process, we can get home. Who is in? Come on, St. Louis! Let's go!"

Now the mood changed at the gate, and people started to smile. A few passengers stood up and clapped. We had momentum. "Okay, here we go. Group one, take your coats off now, get organized, and MOVE!" I stood at the gate and joyfully exchanged high-fives with all the passengers who were moving at a record pace. The passengers' gloomy faces beamed with some excitement as they started to join the program. When the flight boarded, the attendants pulled me aside and said, "We are impressed. We are bumping you up to business class and will give you free drinks for your help. However, we don't think you need those drinks!" I made it happen *and* I made it home that evening.

Your entire mindset and mood can be uplifted and improved if you change your mantra. Sing a song and laugh out loud. Yup. LOL (laugh out loud) and SOL (sing out loud). On another business trip, I had a long weather delay in Houston. I put my phone on speaker and sang loudly at the gate. I soon had an entire family requesting songs and singing along with me. Of course, you don't have to be as dramatic as I am in airports. You can splurge on high-end noise-canceling head-phones or cordless earbuds and listen to music. Music is the playlist of my life and lifts me up every day. Make different playlists for different moods. I have a workout playlist, a relaxing playlist, a romantic playlist, and an energizing playlist.

Run errands in airports. I have purchased clothing, had my makeup done, purchased toiletries, technology, clothes, sunglasses, and gifts. Airports have massage chairs, technology, and book and luggage stores. Research the airports before your flight so you can determine what you can get done while waiting for your departure. Time is of the essence; you can get a multitude of errands completed when you have the downtime to do it. Fill up your rental car with gas when you are not as busy because, inevitably, something will come up before you return it. Also, bookstores in airports are packed with success, psychology, and business books. At least once a month, I purchase a book about how to improve my business, market, manage employees, how to hire, and how to juggle it all. I also read *Success Magazine*, *Harvard Business Review*, and *Entrepreneur Magazine* and catch up on the news. When I return to the office, I share books and magazines with my team. We formed a workbook club, and we took turns presenting these books and topical articles to the rest of the sales team.

I have had some unexpected and significant networking opportunities in airports and on flights. People on flights are often vulnerable and can be open and talkative. Interesting relationships develop when you are seated with a stranger for hours at a time. Sometimes, I do my best to keep to myself by getting into a zone and focusing on clearing my mind. However, there have been many occasions on flights when I have met a passenger on a flight who has connected me to someone who gave me business or who could help me or one of my children with a job opportunity or connection.

Other ways to catch up when traveling relate to what you read, watch, and listen to. The Skimm and other newsletters are a great way to keep up with quick updates of news and sports so you can keep informed while juggling all your other work. Social media is also a great way to follow influencers who advise you with recipes, home décor advice, and fashion tips. Motivational speakers like Gary Vanyerchuk, health advisors like Dr. Jennifer Ashton, and business coaches like Tony Robbins give quick 30-60 seconds of advice that can keep your life well-rounded and armed with tips and tricks to make healthy meals, take care of your health, and change your habits. Find a way to incorporate their suggestions into your own rituals and routines. Listen to podcasts like *The Masterclass Podcast* and load audiobooks onto your mobile devices. When you need downtime, a good movie is also a great way to relax, unwind, and keep balance.

Traveling can destroy your feet. Although I coined a phrase with my female account executives, "heels and deals," do not neglect your feet. Some of my biggest deals were made in high heels. However, I have learned that rocking a great loafer or stylish flat can save you a lot of pain. Neglecting your feet can result in bunions, blisters, plantar fasciitis, and Achilles tendonitis. Women's feet were not meant for high heels! Find a store with a brand that you love that fits your feet and stick with it. If the shoe does not fit like a glove and is uncomfortable in the store, do not buy it! It will only get worse. Do not listen to a salesperson who explains that with time you can "wear in" the shoe to make it more comfortable. An uncomfortable shoe will only get more uncomfortable. My new favorite trend is wearing gym shoes with every outfit, including dresses. There is nothing better than a great pair of fashionable gym shoes. Find a good shoemaker and have the shoemaker put inserts and heel cushions into your shoes or go on Amazon and order shoe inserts and gel pads.

When you drive, I recommend you wear a comfortable flat or gym shoe and bring your heels to change into right before the meeting. I carry a tote to all meetings that can fit my gym shoes so that I can change right before the meetings. Too many city days in the wrong shoes have helped me see the value in this. Finally, when you go to a conference, bring gym shoes or flip-flops to wear while you walk to the event or conference center, and keep the change of shoes in a fashionable bag. You will thank me for this tip. When you come home from a business trip, a foot massage is the perfect way to decompress. These 30-minute treatments will enhance your well-being and help you transition to your busy at-home life without missing a step.

I also believe in investing in good luggage. A good luggage system will expedite your packing, save you time, and keep you organized. If you are constantly on the go, *The Home Edit Life,* by Clea Shearer and Joanna Teplin,[13] is a must-read. In this book, there is an entire section that includes a packing list and an organizational system that I have lived by, which includes packing cubes. Packing systems like the Eagle Creek brand at Target and Amazon have great cube systems and packing options to keep your clothing organized and wrinkle-free. Now, you also have packing and travel systems on Amazon (which I confess to having a serious addiction to) to keep all your toiletries, make-up, and clothing organized. Keep your clothing in these cubes so you do not have to unpack completely. Never put your clothing in the hotel drawers. Also, do not put your suitcase on the hotel floor as you may bring some critters home with you. I keep all of my toiletries and travel essentials in clear, small, zipped bags. This system is detailed in *The Home Edit Life* as they have a section on how to segment and prepare your carry-on and purse, and even how to pack the trunk of your car. I used these systems before they were even a trend. All of my life is accessible. These systems save me time, allowing me to be present with my family more often.

Another great travel tip is to buy two of everything toiletry-related. This double investment will pay off by simplifying your life. Keep one set of toiletries at home, and keep your travel bag packed at all times. This way you have a travel kit ready to go, allowing you to avoid constantly packing when you go on your trips. Keep your travel clothing

---

[13] Clea Shearer and Joanna Teplin. *The Home Edit Life,* Clarkson Potter, 2020

separated in your closet with outfits put together for business trips. Have travel-sized toothpaste, toothbrush, shampoo, and soap in travel containers ready to go at a moment's notice. When you purchase makeup, buy two of everything and then put one in your home makeup station and one in your travel kit. Makeup does not have to be expensive. Follow Bethenny Frankel's Instagram page to find a plethora of drugstore finds that work just as well as the high-end brands you would find at a department store.

Items to travel with that will SAVE you:

- Phone charger
- Car phone charger
- Stain remover wipes: Tide sticks
- Advil and other travel-sized medications
- B12: Great for when you are feeling exhausted
- Zinc: Good for preventing illness
- Emergen-C
- Protein bars and small bags of nuts, trail mix, etc. (have you ever been stuck on a flight for hours with nothing to eat? I was on the tarmac in St. Louis for eight hours with *no food*—not fun!)
- Lint roller
- Travel-sized scissors and nail kit packed in your luggage as they will not pass through security
- Plane sanitizing kit: Get the Lysol spray and Clorox wipes, and when you sit down wipe down your area—tray and the seatbelt included (clearly, this section was written pre-COVID days).

Apps to have loaded on your mobile device:

- Travel apps
- Meditation apps
- Mind Body app: Fitness, salon and spa app
- Uber
- Navigation apps
- Weather apps
- Car wash apps
- Venmo
- Shipt
- Headspace
- ProTracker calorie counter or Weight Watchers
- Daily Ab workout
- Yoga app

When in doubt, throw it out! Curb the chaos in your life by decluttering. *The Home Edit Life* authors Shearer and Teplin also have a TV series that shows you "how to live the life you love without feeling bad about the things you own." What I love is that they advocate starting small and working your way to larger projects. I soothe myself when feeling stressed by organizing a drawer, a closet, or the pantry. I decompress and find peace, joy, and calm in my life by tackling organizing projects. Nothing calms my soul more than an organized closet or drawer. Donating items to charities you believe in will make this process even more fulfilling. Label everything. The most difficult obstacle to being organized is that you can't find your phone, your chargers, or your credit cards. By labeling everything with a label maker, you will find what you need.

Decluttering on the weekends or for ten-minute blocks in the evenings will improve your weekdays. Have a friend or family member help you. When going through your closet, ask two questions: "Have I worn this during the year? Would Lisa wear this?" (Think of your most fashionable friend and add her name instead of Lisa). If the answer is no to both, donate it! Marie Kondo it. Marie Kondo is a Japanese organization consultant who has a TV show and book—*The Life-Changing Magic of Tidying Up*[14]—that discusses keeping only the items that spark joy in your life. Does the clothing item bring you joy? Keep a box in your closet, and when you buy something new, make it mandatory to give away something you do not wear. Less is more. Although I am not a minimalist, I know that by donating clothing items, I will have more peace. Also, eliminating clutter in my home and making sure each space has a feng shui vibe simplifies my life. Feng shui is a practice based on the idea that your environment should harmonize with your internal energy. My stepdaughter, Sydney, has made her mantra, "Protect your peace." I protect my peace at all costs. I will not allow clutter, negative energy, or stress to enter my Zen Zone. Spend time and just *be* home, *be* present, and *be* supportive of those around you.

Being present in the moment needs to be a goal. Finding a way to digitally detox will create more balance in your lives and your families'

[14] Kondō, Marie, and Cathy Hirano. *The Life-Changing Magic of Tidying up: The Japanese art of decluttering and organizing*, Thorndike Press, 2015.

lives. If you are a mom of school-aged kids, set timers for your kids' devices and limit their screen time. Wait as long as you can to give your child a smartphone. Eliminate phone use during meals and keep a basket in your kitchen for the kids to place their devices in while doing their homework. Timers help so that you can let them have breaks every half hour to have five minutes on the phone.

Another type of decluttering relates to the content you let enter your life and your children's lives. The 24-hour news cycle pumps all kinds of negative images and doomsday stories into our already filled-to-capacity brains. You have 100 percent complete control over what comes into your life and your feed. Protect yourself and protect your kids. There is a difference between being informed about current events and politics and the inundation of sensationalized news, fake news, and too-much-of-everything news. Human brains were not created or devised to intake so much negative news. So what is the solution? The solution is boundaries, filters, and phone rules. Our world has become divisive and scary. You need to limit what comes into our small world, as you cannot control what is happening in the big world. However, putting our heads in the sand is not a viable option. Put apps and limits on your children's phone usage, as well as social media accounts, to monitor what your kids have access to.

Like any tool, both the internet and social media should be used strategically and sparingly. Balance is everything. Finding the proper balance in your life by having phone-free interactions and by setting time limits, and establishing strict rules for your children about how they use their devices and social media will help you raise evolved, healthy children. My client and friend, famous trial attorney Troy Rafferty, recently advocated, "Take a day and put your phone away." I challenge all of you to do this. Wait as long as you can to give your kids phones and allow them on social media platforms. Too much exposure to social media can affect your health and the health of your children.

Prioritize your health and take it seriously. Many working moms often put their own health last. In order to find balance, it is crucial to find good doctors and to get regular health checkups. These should include the dentist, the dermatologist for annual or bi-annual skin checks, and an internist to monitor your blood work. When I started my company and was on the road every week, I started feeling sick. I exercised regularly at the gym, had a relatively healthy diet, and took long walks. I visited several doctors before I found one who ran the proper blood tests. I found out that I was a diabetic. My fatigue and other issues were related to this condition. It took several years to regulate my blood sugar and learn how to manage this chronic condition. Do not take your health for granted. Start young and get to the doctor regularly. If you do not think the physician is the right fit, see several doctors until you find the right one. When you work and manage a busy family, you often put your own health on the back burner. Letting your health deteriorate will cause issues for your entire family and your work team.

Finally, it is okay to say no to a business trip or work commitment when you have a moment of dread. Listen to your inner voice when it tells you to say no to a commitment or cancel an important trip. One of the most poignant moments as a working mom is that moment when you have a work commitment that interferes with a "mom" moment, and you need to choose between the two. My moment of dread, or at least one of them, occurred when my oldest son was not feeling well. He had just been diagnosed with Crohn's disease and was slowly recovering and adapting to life with a new normal. His father was out of town and was flying back while I had to fly on a small plane in an ice storm to present to a very prestigious law firm in a small southern town. Before leaving that day, I rocked my morning by packing lunches and backpacks, organized pickups and carpools for all their activities, and then got all three kids on the bus. It was a proud mom moment, and I felt good about not forgetting anyone's lunches or permission slips.

As my son was about to leave the house for the bus stop, he informed me he had a terrible pain in his stomach. I gave him some Motrin and put him on the bus. He had been complaining of pain and had been hospitalized several weeks earlier, so I had a feeling these were not just gas pains. Then, my daughter, knowing I was leaving, started to whine and complain that she did not want to go to school that day. This work meeting was incredibly important, as it was an account that I had tried to land for years. I was prepared for my presentation—packed, and ready to go. I took a car service to the airport, and while rolling my carry-on through the busy airport to my gate at O'Hare, I saw flights being canceled because of the inclement weather. However, my flight was scheduled to leave on time.

As I watched the plane being de-iced, I had that mom's moment of dread and knew that leaving my kids was not the best choice. Even though the kids had backups while I was away, if they needed anything,

I also knew and felt that a substitute mom would not suffice. As the flight was about to board, I called a friend to pick me up and left the airport without my luggage. The kids were fine. The meeting was canceled. I did not get that account that year. I did *not* care. At the end of the day, my greatest accomplishment is my three kids. I will never look back and think that I missed landing that big account. I will look back and think that I rocked being a mom and raised healthy, happy, and successful children.

Traveling for work is exhausting. It is imperative to create balance at home. There is no crying at work. Do not take emotions to the workplace. Vent to your friends and then show up 100 percent. Show up all day and all the way. Focus on the job at hand and put all emotions to bed while at work. What do I do when I have days where I am run down, sad, stressed, or cannot pull it together, you may ask? On those days, I take the day off from work, call my best friend, and meet her at the beach or the park for a long walk. When you feel the need to run, this means you are probably run down from lack of sleep and lack of friend time. Listen to your body. Take breaks.

The place and environment where you work are important. If you surround yourself with beauty and comfort, this will help you to be successful. Do not stick to the nine-to-five. I am a morning person and often have my best creative spurts when I am awake before anyone else, and can work alone while staring out the window. Looking at nature can spur creative juices. If you do not have any nature scenes to look at, then purchase some artwork for your office so that you can look at something beautiful. I am in the process of collecting antique art of beautiful needlepoint floral bouquets. The search for the artwork is just as fun as looking at it on my office wall.

Brené Brown discusses the embracing of "joy" in your life in her book *The Gifts of Imperfection: Let Go of Who You Think You're Supposed to Be and Embrace Who You Are.*[15] I decided to come up with a list to determine what fosters joy for me. First, find a quiet place where you can sit and just be. Then, get a computer out or a beautiful notebook and a pen and compose your joy list. Here is mine:

- Date nights with my husband
- Watching the sunset at the beach
- Beach walks
- Friend time
- Listening to music
- Writing
- Poetry

Now, the key part is making the time—right now—on your calendar to make your own joy list. Then **make it happen**. I set up a night where my husband surprised me and took me out, and we knocked out much of my joy list on one date night. We went to the beach, where we watched the sunset, ate at our favorite Italian place, and then went to a beach bar where I programmed all our favorite songs on the digital jukebox. This spontaneous evening filled my cup and sustained me for a while. Also, the evening was made even more special as Jim put his

---

[15] Brené Brown. *The Gifts of Imperfection: Let Go of Who You Think You're Supposed to Be and Embrace Who You Are*, Random House, 2010

phone away and we were fully present with each other. Think of being fully present as the best present you can get from someone.

Traveling for work can be challenging. However, if you create the right network and environment around you, prepare for travel with lots of travel hacks, and keep yourself grounded while at home, you can make whatever you want in life happen. Set boundaries around your travel, and when you come home, unwind, relax, and be present. Watching your children evolve, being present in their lives, and owning your truth when that moment of dread hits is a key component for working moms. When you look back at your life, you will never regret the one meeting you did not attend. You will reflect on your accomplishments, and you will know that your children are truly the greatest legacy you can leave. By fostering values, setting a good example, giving back, finding joy in everyday moments, and involving your kids in what you do, your legacy will always be the greatest gift of all: your family and your children.

Top 5 Travel Tips for Busy Working Women:

1. Use time while flying to be creative.
2. Take good care of your feet and buy comfortable shoes.
3. Invest in good luggage.
4. Keep two of everything for your toiletry bags.
5. Declutter often.

CHAPTER 5

STEPPING STONES: UNRAVEL TO REBUILD

❝ ————————————

*"The way you recreate your
life can be powerful."*

———————————— **❞**

The sale of Momentum Funding coincided with a time when my children were more independent, and it was time for me to move forward. I am not sure that having it all is possible. I do not feel that you can juggle all the moving parts without letting something go. In my journey, I have met many other working mothers and fathers who have sacrificed a lot for their careers. The harder they work, the more they lack balance. The more successful their businesses are, the less balance they have at home. Something usually must give. For many people, the "something" is their marriage.

I have helped many women through bad breakups, toxic marriages, and dysfunctional relationships. It is incredibly difficult, if not impossible, to fix a damaged relationship. What I have learned is that it is imperative to work on your marriage before something devastating pops up because it will. A marriage counselor once told me that if your marriage is built on quicksand, it will collapse. Build a strong collaborative foundation to make sure that when life gets difficult, your relationship can weather the storms.

It is important to choose wisely when deciding to marry. If you are a woman starting off in the launching pad phase of life, it is important to make good decisions that follow your inner voice. Use your intuition and innate knowledge to follow your heart. According to authors John Gottman and Nan Silver in *The Seven Principles for Making Marriage Work,*[16] the key to a successful marriage is that they are "based on deep friendship." Many of us live in our heads and rationalize with checklists instead of listening to the voice inside us that knows what the right decisions are. Most divorced women or men knew at the time they were married that something was missing in the relationship. They compromised and pushed down their intuition, rationalizing that they could change the person or the behaviors that they did not like in their partner.

One of the most important decisions you make in life is who you marry. This is not a decision to be taken lightly. Make sure that your values align with your partner. Communicate often and early. See a marriage counselor or religious or spiritual advisor before marriage and regularly ask each other difficult questions. You will not agree on

---

[16] Gottman, John, Nan Silver. *Seven Principles for Making Marriage Work,* United States: Harmony, 2015

everything. However, how you work through these difficult conversations will set the groundwork for the challenges that will inevitably arise in your marriage. Do not compromise by marrying someone who does not meet your needs in the early years.

Do the work early and often before there is a crack in the foundation of your relationship. The effort you put into your marriage now will help you prevent issues later on. There are several books that espouse theories for marital satisfaction that I highly recommend. First, it is important to understand your attachment style. *Attached* by Amir Levine and Rachel Heller[17] is an incredible resource for learning how to evolve and work on your relationship. The authors break down the three styles of attachment: secure, anxious, and avoidant. Then they take a deep dive into how these attachment styles affect relationships. Finding a compatible partner, working on respect, and filling your partner's emotional cup based on how he or she attaches, will lead to a more fulfilling partnership. Another way that knowing your attachment style can help is by learning to be more comfortable with intimacy by breaking negative patterns from your past and by healing prior wounds. Understanding attachment styles can offer significant benefits for individuals and their relationships. By understanding how you interact, you can foster self-awareness, which will lead to healthier and more intentional responses to your partner. Also, once you take a deep dive into these attachment theories, you will have more empathetic communication and can articulate your needs more effectively.

---

[17] Levine, Amir and Heller, Rachel S. F., *Attached*, TarcherPerigee, 2012.

Once I spent the time learning about attachments, I understood I had an avoidant style. When I was in a disagreement with my spouse, I often felt "an irrepressible need to bolt." By understanding why I felt that way, I am now able to explain that I need space and time to process the issues before we can effectively work on them. Also, I make a relationship gratitude list to remind myself to think of all the positive things about my spouse and find ways that my partner makes me happy instead of making lists of the negative things. As a true romantic, I have a belief in soul mates. I now understand that true soul mates are people who come into your life at the right time; when you are ready, you will allow this person to get close to you because of the work you do on yourself through enlightenment and knowledge.

Overall, understanding attachment styles helps individuals cultivate more meaningful, supportive, and resilient romantic relationships. However, new theories of relationships have offered a more modern perspective that adds to this theory. Psychologist Dené Logan's groundbreaking book *Sovereign Love*[18] has suggested that the way masculine and feminine energy can be skewed in a relationship can contribute to the demise of a marriage and can be a predictor of divorce. Not only do attachment styles contribute to marital discord, but women who take on more of the masculine energy in the relationship can often feel resentful and misunderstood. I know I took on a masculine role in my family dynamic. This skewed energy fostered discord and resentment. However, at the time, I did not express or understand how I felt. If you

---

[18] Logan, Dené. *Sovereign love: A guide to healing relationships by reclaiming the masculine and feminine within.* United States: Sounds True, 2024.

are unable to articulate your resentments and avoid difficult conversations, you can create a void that cannot be repaired.

Sometimes you are working with a partner who has many issues under the surface, and you will not be able to effectively communicate unless you get deeper. The iceberg theory is a behavior model that states that a person's behavior can "only be properly understood in the context of the factors that caused it. What a person does is the "tip of the iceberg"—what we don't see are the emotional, cultural, and other factors that lie beneath the surface and cause that behavior."[19] Rick Plasket, a business coach I work with, has helped me use this theory to work on my relationships with my husband and to work with team members in business.

Another well-known tool for marital satisfaction is the Gottman Method, developed by doctors John and Julie Gottman. After studying relationships for more than 40 years, they offer helpful strategies for improving relationship satisfaction, minimizing marital stress, and avoiding conflict. The book *The Seven Principles for Making Marriage Work*[20] provides practical advice to build and grow love, trust, and intimacy. In this groundbreaking work, Dr. Gottman hypothesizes that what makes marriages work is that happy couples have learned how to keep their negative thoughts and feelings about each other from overwhelming the positive ones. He says these marriages are emotionally

---

[19] Verity, Hollis. "Understanding the Iceberg Theory of Behavior." *HealthyPlace*. July 26, 2021. https://www.healthyplace.com/blogs/copingwithdepression/2021/7/understanding-the-iceberg-theory-of-behavior.

[20] Gottman, John, Silver, Nan. *Seven Principles for Making Marriage Work,* United States: Harmony, 2015

intelligent and are the biggest predictor of success for a relationship. Besides books about the Gottman Method, I recommend Gottman apps on your phone (Gottman Card Decks), workshops, couples' retreats, podcasts, conferences, and one-on-one sessions with Gottman-trained therapists.

Another key theory of the Gottman Method relates to the four horsemen—criticism, contempt, defensiveness, and stonewalling—or communication issues that can predict the demise of a relationship. Contempt is when one partner disrespects the other by conveying a sense of superiority over the other. Stonewalling is when a partner is frustrated by the criticism and the contempt, becomes defensive, and then retreats by tuning the other partner out. Recognizing these toxic behaviors during an altercation and replacing them with respect, appreciation, and "I" instead of "you" statements will alleviate the stress that occurs during an argument. In addition, taking responsibility for your part in the issue and knowing when you are emotionally overwhelmed so you can take a break to calm yourself down also allows for robust communication. Laughter and over-communicating help. Regular rituals and date nights help intimacy. Understand each other's triggers and emotions. Learn from the situation rather than letting resentment build up. Regularly express empathy, appreciation, and affection, and find small, meaningful ways to say thank you or show love.

My husband Jim and I have regular monthly sessions with a trained Gottman Method communication expert. In addition, we have weekly check-ins. We practice what I am preaching. I will not allow the four horsemen to creep into our relationship. Learning about attachment theories and working on relationships has made me more self-aware as a wife, mother, sister, friend, and daughter. I know it is working because my sister Jennifer recently complimented me. She said that when she offered me constructive criticism, I listened and did not get defensive. These skills are like any skills that you learn. They must be actively practiced daily until they become part of your life. Building self-awareness and emotional intelligence by working on your marriage and yourself to prevent issues will allow you to have a healthy partnership.

Just like people see internists for health check-ups and meet with lawyers for estate planning, meeting with a counselor, a pastor, or a spiritual leader for help with your relationship before there is an issue will help you avoid failing. My husband and I have learned how to communicate effectively and help each other rephrase our words. This ensures that our conversations are productive, kind, and straightforward. We work daily on our communication; we invest the time and energy necessary for our marriage to thrive. Through this method, my husband and I have been able to work through our differences. We communicate in a healthy way with respect and love. We have learned how to counter contempt, resolve conflict, and share insights into our dreams and aspirations for the next phase of life. Shared rituals help us prioritize our marriage. These strategies will build a strong foundation, enhance marital satisfaction, and ensure that negative interactions do not undermine us. Through consistent practice and forming healthy habits, you can create a more resilient and fulfilling partnership. Just as you put all of your effort into your work, it is necessary and more important to put the hard work into your marriage.

Life presents complex and painful challenges. If your relationship is not strong enough, you are not equipped with robust communication skills, and you lack the proper tools, you will not make it through to the other side. I am not someone who accepts failure. I fight through adversity with a "make it happen," "glass-half-full" attitude (*Sapiens* is a fantastic book that discusses more in-depth that philosophy). I am a fixer. I tried for years to help my first marriage, but in the end, it did not succeed. Usually, by the time you wake up and realize that the marital foundation has cracks, the fracture is too deep to heal.

For everyone I know who is no longer married, their marriages fell apart years before the actual break up. Most of these people will tell you they knew early on that the intimacy was missing. When kids are involved, it is complicated. Ways to prevent issues that will come up for working moms all involve dads and husbands who are 100 percent invested in being 50/50 partners to share the workload in the home. The relationship can suffer if the male does not take on household and parenting roles (including carpools, activities, meal planning, and grocery shopping). There are also households where the woman works outside of the house, and the husband or partner is the stay-at-home parent. I do not want to stereotype.

Communication needs to happen often and early in the marriage, and the traditional roles of women and men need to shift significantly in a home where both parents work. I am happy when I see my son cooking and grocery shopping for his fiancée, Lindsey. I love that they have deep affection and frequent healthy communication. If you add religion and spirituality to your marriage and your family, this will strengthen the bond when the going gets tough. I am elated that young couples have learned how to share the workload in their homes. I am hopeful and confident that this trend will continue. If you are someone who does not have an evenly distributed parenting and housework schedule with your spouse or partner, making changes now will prevent issues later on. There is nothing more important than sharing responsibilities in the home. Communication is crucial and needs to be frequent and scheduled. Life will get in the way. If you do not have weekly discussions, you will allow all of life's roadblocks to take priority, and before you know it, your relationship will suffer.

A friend recently said to me, "People who get divorced do not believe in marriage." I know she did not mean to be hurtful, and I appreciated her candor in speaking her truth. We have friends who suffered through painful betrayals and difficult times, including health and substance abuse issues. Several of these couples have worked through these hardships and are still together. The question is, are they happy together? Are they together for the right reasons? Staying together for the kids is not healthy if you are miserable and in an abusive or passionless marriage. If the marriage becomes more work than fun, this is a sign that you need to take a deep look at the underlying issues. Unfortunately, most couples who divorce wait too long before going through the process because they do not want to admit failure or hurt the kids. The problem is that by waiting too long, usually one or both partners have left the marriage in some way—physically or mentally.

Gwyneth Paltrow used the phrase "conscious uncoupling"[21] in 2014 when she and her then-husband, Chris Martin, announced their separation. It refers to a cooperative and respectful approach to the ending of a marriage. The idea is that both partners separate with limited conflict and emotional damage to focus on mutual respect and co-parenting positively with self-awareness. Another celebrity, Kate Hudson, has a fluid vision of marriage and family that can help us move into a more forward-thinking mindset around the age-old institutions of marriage and family. Kate, who has three children from three different relationships, said in *People Magazine*,[22] "Love can change form. It's interesting when you have that modern family; there's so much love for all the kids… It's beautiful… it's the most mature thing for the kids." I hope we can progress to a time where the end of a marriage is not looked at as a failure. A 50-year marriage fraught with arguments, lack of passion, and negative energy is not a success just because the couple made it to the finish line. A successful marriage is one where the couple faces challenges and makes it through tough times with active communication, intimacy, counseling, spirituality, passion, laughter, and compassion. Laughter is the anecdote for longevity in a relationship. When the laughter ends, the marriage often falters.

Mara Bernstein is a prominent divorce attorney in Boca Raton, Florida, and the founder of Pivot With Us. She has a law firm that promotes Divorce Different™, which focuses on finding a better way to

---

[21] "Conscious Uncoupling," *Goop*, March 25, 2014, https://goop.com/wellness/relationships/conscious-uncoupling-2/.
[22] Nelson, Jeff. "Why Kate Hudson Was 'Afraid' to Pursue Lifelong Music Dream: 'I'm Just Going to Do It,'" *People Magazine*, May 27, 2024

navigate the end of a marriage. Pivot With Us is a business Mara founded specializing in crafting transformative retreats set in luxurious, nature-filled surroundings. Her mission is to empower women to discover clarity, build community, and gain the insights they need to live their best lives. Mara quotes Oprah Winfrey when she states, "Challenges are gifts that force us to search for a new center of gravity. Don't fight them. Just find a new way to stand."[23] Mara herself faced many challenges in her life, including the death of a child and her husband. She now spends her time helping people divorce differently. She says that the dilemma is always, "Should I stay or should I go?" However, usually, when someone consults with a divorce lawyer, the answer is that they should have gone a long time before that meeting.

Divorce can be scary for most people, especially for women who have stayed at home with the children for years and who have little or no insight into their finances. Women often give up careers, making sacrifices to help their husbands and families. These women often feel fear and significant financial insecurity when they do not have knowledge of or access to their finances and do not have the ability to support themselves. Also, many women feel ashamed to share with Mara that they do not have information about or control of their finances. It wasn't until 1964, with the Civil Rights Act, that women could legally open their own bank account. Therefore, we have to give ourselves some grace. Mara said, "Women should not feel shame around not having controlled their finances. Most couples divide the household roles, and most men handle the financial responsibilities."

---

[23] Winfrey, Oprah. *What I Know For Sure*. Macmillan, 2014

The role women play in their marriage is impactful, even if it does not involve financial control.

Although it is important to not feel shame if you lack knowledge of your finances, financial independence is imperative. I cannot tell you the number of women who are not involved in their financial well-being, including doctors, lawyers, and CEOs. I was not interested in the finances of my family. I never had a budget and did not get involved in my investments. My ex-husband and I had split up the family tasks. I oversaw the kids' education, grocery shopping, home décor, and all matters relating to the children while he managed the traditional role of banking, bills, and finances.

My advice to young women starting out is that you should partner in everything. Traditional roles should be shut down. Partner with your spouse to make holistic decisions about all monetary decisions. Have regular family meetings to discuss all issues you are jointly handling. A weekly or bi-weekly meeting with your partner is very important. This will also help your marriages or relationships by creating open communication and transparency about all areas that affect you, your spouse, and your children. Communication is the key to a good relationship. All major financial decisions should be handled collaboratively. Join a finance club, educate yourself with emails like Skimm Money, and watch TV programs that discuss money and finances. Even if you are not interested, there are ways to make this part of your life fun and engaging.

Another reason both parties fear separation and divorce is because they are concerned about the emotional well-being of their children.

Mara asserts, "It is not the divorce that affects the kids; it is the way people divorce and how we model conflict resolution and respect." She also states, "You need to love your kids more than you hate each other." Couples should have both pre- and postnuptial agreements in order to prepare. Finally, she says, "Divorce is difficult. It doesn't have to be devastating. Who you marry is who you marry. Once you start to try to change that person, it will foster resentment." The end of a marriage is often the beginning of a new way of life and can be very liberating as you reinvent yourself to live a more authentic life.

I hope that instead of society looking at divorce as a failure, we will look at this new chapter as a stepping stone for living more authentically. No one can or should judge another couple on their marriage. Staying together after infidelity or any kind of marital discord is only admirable if major work is done. Remaining in a marriage to keep the status quo or for the kids who will grow up and leave the nest to create their own lives is not healthy. Staying because you truly love the person and want to work to make your relationship as strong and beautiful as possible makes sense. Your partner should be your best friend, grow with you, and support your dreams and career aspirations.

Living authentically sometimes requires people to separate to live their lives with purpose. People can make the wrong choices because of timing and circumstances, and life can get in the way. Just because you chose to marry someone, and it does not work out, does not mean that you failed. It also does not mean that you do not believe in marriage. It means that you love yourself enough and love your family enough to show them that you can recreate a beautiful life. It means that you are strong and brave enough to move forward to forge a different, more authentic path for yourself. It means that you want to show your children how to love in a healthy way and want to model a healthy relationship for them. It is never a failure when you have children. Moving on is okay. You will be okay. You can **make it happen** and recreate your life to be anything and everything you want it to be.

The pain of a marriage ending is in the loss of the family, the deep core of the connection to the babies that you created together. It is all incredibly difficult, and I do not want to try to glamorize or trivialize the ending of a marriage. What I want to stress is that after the heartache, you will grow and move on. Life will normalize. You will look back at that relationship as a learning journey and the evolution of the person you are becoming. That does not mean the memories you have are going to fade away. You will keep them in a place where you can go back and feel them. Healthy relationships with your ex-spouse will then create new family units that will thrive when both parties are finally happy and at peace.

How you recreate your life can be powerful. At a recent conference, two women approached me and asked me what it would feel like for them on the other side. The truth is that the decision is incredibly complicated. There will be good days and bad days. I do not want to glamorize divorce. However, I want to eliminate the stigma and shame around divorce; it is okay if you have tried to work on your marriage and realize that no work will revive the relationship. Move forward. Move on. *Make it happen.*

Is it easy to have it all as a working mother? My answer is emphatically *no*. Many strong, intelligent, powerhouse women have shared the struggles of their marriages with me. They are often on top of their game at work. These women confide that although they are successful at juggling their home lives and children, they struggle to put the time into their marriages that is needed for them to thrive.

I interviewed several professional women at different points in their lives for this book. Each woman had a similar story. They had satisfying and fulfilling careers. These women knew when they married their husbands that there was something missing. They thought that they could change the men. The women knew that they had the drive to be successful, and they also knew that staying at home with kids and rocking the domestic world would not give them the satisfaction they needed. These women were pursuing higher education and had already started their careers when they met their husbands. They also knew they wanted children and wanted to be mothers. They thought that they could have it all. They married men who they thought would be good fathers and who checked all the boxes for them when the timing was ripe and their biological clocks were ticking. The men were proud to tell people about their high-achieving, professional wives who traveled to speaking engagements and who men looked up to. They loved the income these women brought into the family. It all seemed too good to be true, and at some point, it became obvious that it was. Then the house of cards came crashing down. The work was not done early on.

You cannot run a family, a successful business, and also have a perfect marriage. You see, perfection is not obtainable unless sacrifices are made and hard work is done early in the relationship. Marriage does not occur in a vacuum. Each partner needs to understand their past and their partner's triggers for the relationship to stay the course. When 25- to 30-year-olds get married, they often want to have children quickly. Marriages fail when the couple lacks a solid foundation of love and the proper channels for clear communication. They do not understand each other's love languages and fail to have clear and concise expectations of what the give and take will be in their relationship. Once children enter the equation, the marriage will falter even more. I have seen this countless times.

Although my observations are not based on empirical evidence, they are all so similar that I can only surmise that we are seeing a pattern. We need to break this pattern. The trend now is for young men to support their new wives and new mothers in a more robust and healthy way. With paternal leave, with both partners sharing in the domestic chores in the home, and with more women in the workforce, I am optimistic that the future is brighter for young men and women who are high achievers and want to have collaborative relationships and share equally in the domestic roles. Young couples need to encourage each other to find the most important part of every relationship. They need to create a safe space to have a work-life balance.

My goal is not to be the "divorce whisperer." I want to guide women and men to make good decisions when choosing their spouses. I want to encourage couples to do the hard work that relationships require before the marriage fails. I want to help individuals believe in themselves enough to not settle, to not feel rushed into marriage, and to make sure that when you pick a life partner, you choose with both your head and your heart. I want you to know that if the decision does not work out, it is okay to move on and that you will be okay. What is not okay is living in an inauthentic way because you are worried about the kids or what other people will think. If you are making life decisions now, follow that inner voice. You will never doubt yourself when you follow your truth.

Top 5 Ways to Keep a Marriage and Partnership Healthy:

1. Check in weekly with your spouse to make sure you are both on the same page.
2. Plan weekly date nights to spend alone time with your spouse.
3. Over-communicate and do not hold anything back when you speak to each other.
4. Share parenting roles and all the chores at home equally.
5. Walk away and take a break when you feel overwhelmed and flooded, and come back to speak to your spouse when you are feeling more calm.

CHAPTER 6

"PRIME TIME": PIVOTAL MOMENTS

"

"Being alone is an art and to find true peace in the present, it is imperative to master it."

"

Forget the terms "midlife crisis" and "empty nest syndrome." You need to eliminate these concepts and negative phrases to recreate a whole new positive dialogue and vernacular around this "prime time" of your life. I had a midlife crisis and experienced sadness and loss when I was faced with an empty nest. I now realize that these crises were simply my turning point and the beginning of how I could reinvent myself to become a better, more relaxed, and evolved person and move into the next phase of life with grace, energy, emotional intelligence, and a positive outlook. I could **make it happen** and reverse the negativity and sadness that those outdated terms represented. Rephrasing, adjusting, and renewing are all part of the new "prime time" for our lives.

Once I divorced and remarried, it was now time for a new, exciting chapter. After selling Momentum Funding and exiting the company, I decided to retire. My children were basically on autopilot. Andrew was engaged to an incredible woman, Lindsey, and lived in Chicago. He was an entrepreneur and founded a technology company. Jacob lived in Austin, Texas, and was successful in his career with a legal software company. Ashley graduated from the University of Wisconsin, moved to Chicago, and worked as an analyst for a global digital ad agency. All three kids had successful career and life paths. I accomplished what I had worked so hard for so many years to achieve. My children did not need me as regularly. There were fewer frantic phone calls. There were no more visits to college campuses. The years of raising my children were over, as all three were settled in their adult lives. I was on the road for so many years, and they were the years of them coming and going and of moving in and moving out. For ten straight years, I had kids in college without a year off. When they graduated, I helped them move into their apartments to start their adult lives. There was always another kid right behind the other. When I traveled to Austin to move Jacob into his apartment and then a few years later to Chicago to move my baby into her adult apartment downtown, I cried when I left them—I enjoyed being needed. Yet, if you create and foster independent children, you have done an incredible job. Training your children to not rely on you is the greatest gift and the biggest accomplishment you can have.

Now it was finally time for me! Happily remarried to my husband, Jim, we traveled and had a beautiful home life. Family and friends surrounded us, and all was good in the world. I took tennis and golf lessons, met friends for dinners, got involved with charities, and figured this would be enough. For me, it was not. I felt isolated and alone, with countless hours in the day and very little to keep me busy. I was used to running a company, working full time, traveling for work, and managing more in a day than most people handle in a month. I quickly realized that in this new phase of life, I could not just completely cut off that driven and motivated side of me. I could not detach and say goodbye so quickly to that cerebral and chaotic way of life. I felt malaise now that my adult children did not need me as much, and also a significant loss, as I no longer had a team of employees who relied on me for career and life advice.

The empty nest syndrome is attributed to Dorothy Canfield Fisher,[24] a sociologist who used this phrase to describe the loss and loneliness that parents, especially mothers, feel when their children leave home. The more independent and capable my children became, the more sadness, loss, and loneliness I felt. My identity was also connected to my career and leadership role at work for two decades. Without work and with the kids gone, I was at a complete loss. I realized that although my husband was a huge support for me during this time, I could not rely on him alone for my happiness. I had to reinvent myself at this new stage of life and find purpose and meaning. Another challenge for women during this phase of life is that often we have to care for our aging parents. My father was diagnosed with Parkinson's disease, and I quickly had to step in and support my parents on a daily basis. Just as the kids are independent, our parents become needy and

---

[24] Canfield, Dorothy. *Mothers and Children (1914)*, Reprinted: Kessinger Publishing, 2008

often rely on our constant support and intervention during their senior years. However, although I was busy with my parents, this care did not replace my need to be productive, and I craved a distraction even more.

At this midlife point, there is a new phenomenon called "failure to launch,"[25] in which some kids refuse to leave home and continue to be dependent on their parents. During the course of writing this book, I experienced this phenomenon myself. My stepdaughter came home from college after a few days and has now moved in with us full-time to attend a local school. I am grateful that we have the resources and have done the foundational work to ensure we can manage this phase with grace and love. This has become a very painful issue for many parents who struggle as their children root themselves in their childhood bedrooms.

As much as I lament the empty nest, having adult children living with you has its own unique challenges. Slightly over half of the 18- to 29-year-olds live at home with their families.[26] Finances and mental health issues play a large role in this migration home or failure to leave. This dynamic adds yet another layer of strain to already stressed-out parents. Marriages are affected as the parents do not always agree on how they will set boundaries and push their adult children.

---

[25] "When Kids Fail to Launch as Adults." *Wall Street Journal*, October 3, 2022.

[26] Pew Research Center. (2020, September 4). *A majority of young adults in the U.S. live with their parents for the first time since the Great Depression.* https://www.pewresearch.org/fact-tank/2020/09/04/a-majority-of-young-adults-in-the-u-s-live-with-their-parents-for-the-first-time-since-the-great-depression/

Working with a therapist who can help parents foster greater independence and financial stability in their children is one strategy for addressing this challenging issue. Additionally, working with adult children to help them conquer their fears can provide the momentum needed for them to become independent and grow. More importantly, encouraging adult children to take responsibility for their own futures is a critical component. A must-read for both parents and adult children is Meg Jay's groundbreaking book, *The Defining Decade: Why Your Twenties Matter—And How to Make the Most of Them Now.*[27] Jay explains the reasons adult children return home, their struggle to form significant relationships, and their lack of drive and purpose. She offers solutions to help parents understand this generation and helps twentysomethings understand themselves. Forming a support group with other parents facing similar challenges can also be beneficial.

Just as we did not get an education or roadmap for success for our marriages, we are not trained to handle midlife. The midlife crisis is a real issue for many people, especially for women. I know that my midlife crisis hit just as I was in the midst of building a company, dealing with my adult children, getting divorced, and caring for my father with his debilitating chronic illness. With my innate "glass-half-full" perspective and **make it happen** mantra, I decided to shift my perspective and was able to take a crisis and pivot it to a more positive and renewed way of life. An incredible resource on this phase of life is a book, *Learning to Love Midlife*, by Chip Conley.[28] He rebrands the idea of midlife

---

[27] Meg Jay, *The Defining Decade: Why Your Twenties Matter—And How to Make the Most of Them Now*, updated ed. (New York: Twelve, 2021).
[28] Conley, Chip. *Learning to Love Midlife*, Little Brown Spark, 2024

as "something profound and beautiful." Conley defines this period of life as an awakening inside us and provides knowledge about settling into this transformative journey. He quotes Yale University's Dr. Becca Levy, who shows that when you look at aging more positively, your health, sex life, cognitive functioning, and other areas of your life dramatically improve. Levy shows that shifting our perspective from negative to positive will improve our health and add years to our life.[29]

Redefining midlife and changing your attitude will allow this period of time to be more of an awakening—after the darkness comes light. Conley uses a beautiful analogy to discuss midlife:

> Midday and midlife have a lot in common. Early in the morning, a shadow is cast west. A child dreams about her future. Late in the day, a shadow is cast east. An elder leaves a legacy for future generations. But at midday, with the sun directly overhead, we lose our shadow, just as we may lose our sense of direction in midlife. This is a temporary condition, as the afternoon will eventually reemerge, but our midlife circumstances and emotions aren't as predictable as the sun. (Conley, *Learning to Love Midlife*, p. 177)

If you are feeling lost or stuck and feel like you are helping others while losing track of your own needs, this is perhaps the beginning of your soul's evolution. You will see the light at the end of the tunnel when you understand the growth that occurs during this impactful time in your life. At midlife, you are only at halftime in your story. Conley reminds us that the characters in the *Sex and the City* sequel are the same age as

---

[29] Conley, *Learning to Love Midlife*, p. 5.

the Golden Girls were when their 1985 TV series was filmed. In fact, three of the Golden Girls were around 50. Also, Aristotle hit the nail on the head when he related that the body is perfect at 35 and the soul reaches perfection at 49. Midlife is a time when you can evolve, when you cherish your relationships more than your material possessions, and when your most intimate relationships are formed from life stressors.

Another groundbreaking book about how women evolve in midlife is *The Upgrade: How the Female Brain Gets Stronger and Better in Midlife and Beyond* by Louann Brizendine.[30] This is a non-fiction book that explores the changes in the female brain during midlife and dispels many of the common myths of aging with a positive perspective on the potential for growth as women age. This stage of life can be freeing as women embrace new opportunities for personal growth. You, too, can reinvent yourself at this stage of life and accomplish the things you have always dreamed of. The amount of time you have once your children are independent, and your career has slowed down, or you have retired will allow you to look back at all of your accomplishments and spend time to find your passion.

The term "empty nest syndrome" connotes a depressing and sad phase of life, and my friends who are experiencing this loss at this stage of life all lament that they are at the end stage of life. You need to rebrand this syndrome as your "prime time." Just as the book *Upgrade* shows that women's brains are at a peak point for personal growth, and

---

[30] Brizendine, Louann, Hertz, Amy. *The Upgrade: How the Female Brain Gets Stronger and Better in Midlife and Beyond.* Harmony Books, 2022

Conley states that aging is our "curriculum for becoming more conscious," a new vernacular for this chapter of our lives is desperately needed. Despite the "crisis" label, research actually shows that you will grow more satisfied with life after age 50. There is a major "upside" to this era.[31] When you can reframe our mindset to a more positive view of this stage of life, you actually add an additional seven and a half years to our lives.[32] The age-old idea about midlife is that it is a disappointing time with "parents passing away, kids leaving home, financial reckonings, changing jobs, changing spouses, hormonal wackiness, scary health diagnoses, addictive behaviors becoming unwieldy, and the stirring of a growing curiosity about the meaning of life."[33] The new perspective on your halftime is that it's an exciting opportunity to rediscover who you are and reinvent yourself.

Instead of looking at this phase of life in a negative way, let's relabel this stage as the "prime time" of your life. It is a "prime time" to use all of your life lessons and experiences to rebrand yourself, recreate, enhance, and embrace your true self. Many of my friends still worry about their adult children. They worry that adult children will not find independence and financial stability. However, it is imperative to step away and let them discover life on their own terms. Allowing them to make mistakes and fail will help them build life skills that foster resilience. Everyone in life is on their own journey, and we need to give children the space and the ability to find their own path. Women at this stage of life should form peer groups to help each other through this transition;

---

[31] Conley, *Learning to Love Midlife*, p. 4.
[32] Conley, *Learning to Love Midlife*, p. 5.
[33] Conley, *Learning to Love Midlife*, p. 8.

the women who have adult children living at home can collaborate with their friends whose children left home and work together to get through this life transition. It is important to keep in perspective that your adult children will continue to struggle and make mistakes on their own journeys. As much as you worry about their decisions, their happiness, and how often you see them, these issues are beyond your control. What you can control is how you live your life, the example that you are to them, your own happiness, and how you encourage, respect, and react to them in their new stage of life.

One challenge during this "prime time" midlife stage is that although you have more alone time, many women experience loneliness. Understanding this phenomenon will help you navigate challenges during this period. Although it is healthy to have quiet time, loneliness is detrimental and shortens life spans. The odd thing about today's society is that although people are connected through digital devices nonstop, we are all very isolated. Life is about connection. I crave physical connection and meetings in person with employees, lunches with friends, and in-person meetings. With all the businesses in our world, the 24-hour news cycle, and phones ringing at all hours, we have lost touch with what really matters. The human element is slipping away while the digitized world is creeping into our minds, souls, and bodies. Being alone is something that should be cherished and nurtured. Many women keep themselves busy so as not to be alone with their thoughts. During the years of working and raising children, there is often not a lot of time to analyze your life decisions and think about your own needs. Midlife is finally your time to take a deep dive into your emotional needs.

At the midpoint of your life, it is important to master the art of alone time. In ten years, you will read this book, and I am sure there will be even more forms of communication that will saturate and populate, congregate, and proliferate. Do you need even more on your plate? Why can't people separate from devices, the vices, the divisive? Being alone is an art, and to find true peace in the present, it is imperative to master it. Having the toolbox for success that I built when working, building companies, and parenting has helped me with this new phase of life. I recommend you use the skills from that toolbox to prioritize balance in this "prime time" of your life. When you have healthy habits and rituals, this time in your life will evolve with purpose.

Surround yourself during this "prime time" with friends and family as much as possible. The theory of Blue Zones is that people live longer and healthier lives when surrounded by a close-knit group of friends and family. Blue Zones are parts of the world where people live longer and healthier lives than the global average. This theory was introduced by Dan Buettner, who researched regions around the world and noticed that in certain areas, there were lower rates of chronic disease and more centenarians. In the Netflix documentary *Live to 100: Secrets of the Blue Zones*,[34] years of studies showed that loneliness reduces life expectancy. The zones where people live the longest are areas where community involvement and friend circles dominate and permeate daily life and where elderly people live with family members. In our society, elderly people are not valued as they are often put out to pasture in retirement and sent to nursing homes to live out their years.

---

[34] Buettner, Dan. Live to 100: Secrets of the Blue Zones, Directed by Clay Jeter, Makemake, Netflix, 2023

The findings from these Blue Zone studies show that diets rich in vegetables and whole grains, a strong sense of community and purpose for elderly people, strong social engagement, and community are all longevity boosters.

One way to use time during the "prime time" of your life is to become more self-aware and emotionally intelligent. Emotional intelligence has come to light as a theory in more recent years and espouses that one who has this type of intelligence can manage and use their emotions to self-regulate and achieve personal and professional goals. If you can hone your skills for self-awareness during your "prime time," you can then use the time to journal and look back at your life to assess what worked and did not work. Major growth can occur during this time period.

"Prime time" is now my time as I find myself with blocks of quiet time. My initial reaction was to fill the time with shopping, errands, and endless to-do lists. I now force myself to use these blocks of time to just be. This has not been easy for someone who spent her life running from meetings to events to games to recitals. So now, I am in my "being still" phase even though I am still working. I use the quiet time to think and, of course, to write. This book is somewhat of a therapy for me. I can look at my life like a puzzle and break it apart piece by piece in order to understand why I was so successful in some areas and struggled in others. I look at life as a journey, and slowing down often to smell the roses helps you gauge where you are at the prime time of your life. Use this new chapter in your life to recreate a new normal, and when you take the time to take a deep dive into your *why*, you will understand your purpose and recreate yourself. Conley summarizes this time this way: "We're not meant to be perfect in life, but we are meant to be whole…You may think you're shattered in midlife, but this is just because life is offering you… the opportunity to… put yourself back together again piece by piece."[35] Sometimes when everything is falling apart, it is actually coming together.

Top 5 Things to Do When Trying to Evolve and Wind Down:

1. Say no.
2. Create boundaries.
3. Follow your gut.
4. Be present with your thoughts.
5. Journal often.
6. Enjoy the silence.

---

[35] Conley, *Learning to Love Midlife*, p. 202.

CHAPTER 7

THE REINVENTION: LEGACY BUILDING

66 ⸺

"By following the three Ps of marketing, you will find your 'what' and 'why,' and your new personal brand and business will evolve."

⸺ 99

As I have now entered this new "prime time" of my life, I have reinvented myself as the antidote for the sadness I was feeling (and my lack of interest in golf and tennis). I took time to hop off the treadmill and used the time to process the next phase of my life. I became more introspective and emotionally intelligent through this process. I knew I wanted to integrate my skill sets and expertise and share this with others. Having had the background of starting and launching two successful legal service brands, I used my knowledge to launch a consulting company, Lawthentic Consulting.

At the same time, my husband, Jim, started a new law firm. My company handled the marketing and branding for his firm. Marketing had changed dramatically as traditional television ads were more expensive, and the digital landscape became saturated. The cost of marketing a personal injury law firm became prohibitive, with national firms entering smaller markets. I pivoted and took a deep dive into branding, digital marketing, and social media, focusing heavily on video strategy and storytelling. I found that strategy both rewarding and successful. Besides Lawthentic Consulting, I launched a podcast called *Balance and the Bar*, which focused on how to brand and how to work and create balance while scaling a business. Of course, all of this was very on-brand for me.

I have had many iterations in my career, and this most recent one has combined my passions and superpowers. As I became a consultant for lawyers and busy professionals to help them archive their legacies, build their brands, and grow their businesses, I realized that there was a need for a more comprehensive consulting program. These business owners needed help with their personal lives. The one common denominator I noticed in profitable law firms and other businesses is that each of the entrepreneurs, or business owners, has thick skin and has suffered adversity. Often, success came because of a difficult journey and challenges these leaders faced. Many of these executives have gone through marital discord and do not know how to unwind. Each of these successful business owners has a high fear factor or tolerance for risk. All my clients have a story of how they became who they are today. In addition, they understand what drives them to be successful. For all, there was a need for a more holistic approach.

I decided that if I was going to make my clients accountable for daily and weekly habits, I must make myself accountable. I needed to practice what I preached, and I knew that with consistency, daily and weekly habits, patience, and trial and error, this book would evolve, my business would grow, and my story would unfold. I synthesized decades of building relationships with lawyers nationwide to form this consulting business and find my passion by helping lawyers build businesses and brands while incorporating balance into their lives. The one consistent theme throughout my career that predicted the success of my businesses was my expertise in building relationships and my skill at branding.

I built a new personal brand for myself to teach clients how to build their own brands and to help you find yours. So, where do you start? Brainstorm a creative name for your new brand. After finding the name for your brand or business, focus on your target audience. Remember to speak *to* your audience. Remember to be *authentic*. Knowing who you want to influence is the key component for the success of your brand. Colors, sounds, photos, Instagram grids of your personal brand icons, and friends who you follow will all be integral for you to find the look and feel for your brand. Start with your story of your *why*, and then fill in all the details. The name, the color, the logo, and the taglines all matter.

Do not cut corners when going through the branding phase. My first company was named Oasis. The vision in my head was that injured clients who had no financial resources needed a safe place to land to wait for their cases to be resolved. Our island, our "oasis," was a haven for them to land while awaiting trial or settlement. My next company, Momentum Funding, was originally supposed to be a workout business. However, when I had to pivot into legal finance again, the name really struck a chord for me. We wanted to assist clients by moving their cases and their lives forward… with momentum. The original brand was "Get Momentum," and the color was a rich shade of purple. While other legal service brands used the blues and greens, we stood out with our bright purple, particularly at conferences. Lawthentic's name evolved because of my search for transparency and my need to surround myself with truly authentic people.

Authenticity is the knowledge that
you are living your truth.

After you come up with a creative name, follow what I have labeled the "three Ps" of marketing: *passion, promotion, publicity,* and *personal influencers.*

Passion

First, you have to have a *passion* for what you do. How do you find your passion? Make a list of everything that brings you joy. If you love photography, take photos and read everything you can about photography. Go back in time to when you were a small child. What were your hobbies? What did you love to do? Reconnect with the part of you that smiled. The child exists in all of us. We only need to find her by remembering what made you feel whole and happy as a child. I loved writing, music, organizing, dancing, and taking photos. Try a new hobby, take walks in nature, join a club, and talk to as many people as possible. Soon, your passion will surface. Read as much as you can about what you are passionate about to continue to chisel away at this passion. Be open to new ideas and let your passion evolve with time and patience.

I was never passionate about legal funding. When I do a deep dive into my *why*, I now realize I did not want to be a lawyer or run a legal finance business. Many of my career aspirations came from my parents' expectations of me. However, I found a way to take what I was passionate about and incorporate it into my businesses. My passion for people, helping others, and marketing fueled the growth of the businesses I founded, Oasis and Momentum. I utilized my people skills and creativity in branding and marketing to help these specialty finance businesses scale and ultimately sell. Assisting clients with their financial challenges also inspired me to infuse passion and motivation into the businesses.

Promotion

It is not enough to find your passion. The second "P" is *promotion*. Next, you must promote this passion. This involves showing off skills and superpowers to highlight your business or personal brand. Promotion includes marketing your business with messaging. A website educates, inspires, and tells your story. A good website will have video, updated photography, press releases, and articles authored by the principals, and will tell your story in a multitude of ways. Link your website to social media channels on every platform and keep content coming out regularly. Build a network of potential clients by engaging with your audience on social channels. Set up speaking engagements and attend events and conferences that are on brand for you. Education is a key component; you need to showcase what sets you apart from competitors to promote yourself effectively. Write a list of why you are different and then highlight this difference in all of your values and marketing strategies. Find speaking engagements and ways to engage with larger audiences and ask others for testimonials and recommendations. Partner and collaborate with other businesses that have the same vision, mission, and values. When you speak, promote yourself with an authentic voice. When your mission highlights your superpowers and adds value to your potential audience, you will achieve your goals when you lean into your passion and then promote yourself authentically.

Publicity

The third "P" for marketing success is *publicity*. If it is not up on social media, it did not happen. It is no longer enough to be passionate about something and to promote it. You then have to publicize it. For example, I sell social media packages and websites to law firms and consult with these firms about their brands. I have a website, a podcast, and social media channels where I actively and consistently promote my business. It is important to publicize the business. By writing this book, launching press releases, and creating a mastermind, we will now publicize what we are doing. By following the three Ps of marketing, you will find your *what* and *why*, and your new personal brand and business will evolve.

Everyone is on their phones constantly, and the best way to be in front of your audience is to target them where they are—on their devices. I truly believe that social media is the future of all marketing. These platforms have and will revolutionize how we conduct and market our businesses. Create a personal brand that reflects your true passions, and work will meld easily into your personal life. Social media will be an important part of this branding. Building an online presence will take time; to work on this, you need to dive in, and you cannot wait to make it perfect. To get started, focus on Instagram, Facebook, and LinkedIn. I believe social media is the most impactful change in marketing that we have had in generations and that it is only going to continue to skyrocket. I predict that in the next ten years, the phone (or some other type of device) will be the only way we receive our marketing messaging. Social media will be saturated soon. It will get more expensive to break into the platforms. Instagram is the platform where I see the most growth.

Personal Influencers

I created my brand by first studying celebrity and influencer brands I was drawn to. When curating your brand, start by thinking about and studying *personal influencers*. Find other personal brands, celebrities, and social media influencers who you admire, and spend considerable time understanding their brand and figuring out what about that brand speaks to you. I have several inspirations and use these influences like a vision board to curate my own personal style and brand. Research should revolve around Instagram platforms, Google, and any platform you enjoy. Pay attention to aesthetics and the feel of the person's brand, and then note what you like and do not like about the feed. The people I follow are women entrepreneurs and mothers.

Reese Witherspoon has created a robust personal brand that I admire. She named her clothing company Draper James after her grandparents, and her brand celebrates her Southern heritage, style, and hospitality. She also founded a book club where she champions strong female authors and protagonists with compelling storytelling. I have been a voracious reader since childhood and love that Reese promotes and supports authors and books. So many people read on tablets and phones now, and I am trying very hard to digitally detox regularly. Sitting down with a cup of tea and a good hardcover book brings me back to childhood. Reese's book, *Whiskey in a Teacup*,[36] is a gorgeous coffee table book where she shares what her childhood in the South taught her "about life, love, and baking biscuits." This book has stories, personal photographs, and recipes. It is a compilation of Reese's passions. Her success has been sprinkled with hardships in her personal life as she has gone through two divorces. She loves family gatherings, tea parties, and a good glass of Southern iced tea. Like me, she enjoys cooking, domesticity, entertaining, and family life. Nothing makes me happier than when my whole family is gathered around a beautifully decorated table.

Reese's book reminds me of a book that has been a mainstay in my life since I was a young mother. The book *Simple Abundance* by Sarah

---

[36] Witherspoon, Reese. *Whiskey in a Teacup: What Growing Up in the South Taught Me About Life, Love, and Baking Biscuits*, Atria Books, 2021

Ban Breathnach[37] features Zen through domesticity. She writes about the "habit of being—the exultation in the present moment" as an exquisite concept that would and could "enrich our lives beyond measure." Her entire book is about her commitment to the cultivation of being and the fact that the art of the every day will create a meaningful life. Prior to social media influencers who highlighted recipes, lifestyles, and quotes of the day, Sarah Ban Breathnach provided me with daily inspirations about the joy, meaning, and fulfillment of the domestic side of life: entertaining, holidays, parenting, mothering, and table settings were interspersed with daily affirmations, quotes from famous and inspirational authors and philosophers, and daily offerings.

For example, in the chapter "The Bath: Secret Haven of Self-Absorption," she promotes the bathroom as a place for private pampering. She then describes how to turn your own bathroom into a spa vacation by surrounding yourself with scented candles, natural sponges, and scrub brushes. In another musing in her book, she states, "Life is not tidy around here today: Schedules are colliding, needs are conflicting, and the house is strewn with real-life refuse, reflecting outwardly the disarray of my mind at the moment." It is interesting that this beautiful book was written in 1995, the year my son Andrew was born. She wrote the book with an organized walkthrough for each day of the year. The book is devoted to "excavating your authentic self... and finding your authenticity in your daily round: the domestic arts, work, beauty, fashion, and personal pursuits that bring contentment."

---

[37] Ban Breathnach, Sarah. *The Simple Abundance: Journal of Gratitude*, Warner Books, 1996

Twenty-eight years later, as I write this book, I am humbled by the influence that Ban Breathnach had on me as a young mother, a working mother, and a mother trying her best to make things happen while the world was spiraling around me. I truly always wanted more while also finding the simplicity, the solitude, and the beauty in the present moment. When I am feeling the stillness of an empty nest, the quiet where once noise resonated, the complacency of contentment where my soul was previously restless, I pick up this book and let it transport me into the present state of being.

Joanna Gaines created Magnolia Table as her personal brand. Her brand encompasses rustic farmhouse vibes, family, and community. Her Hearth & Hand brand for Target revolves around cooking and home decor. Joanna is a mother and businesswoman who works with her spouse and manages a large farm home, five kids, and her business. Her recipes, life advice, cooking show, and décor radiate warmth and connection. She ties in her family throughout her brand. Joanna's story reminds us that it is okay to make mistakes and to bring it all back home. She has done an incredible job of capturing home improvement and lifestyle aesthetics. In her book *Homebody,*[38] Gaines has a theme of "telling your story" within your home. She discusses designing your home "with intention, to surround yourself with items that mean something to you, and choose furnishings and details that make you happy or inspired or contented." Like my life and home, she believes that authenticity is about a home that constantly evolves. I have spent my days off since I was a young mother in antique malls and thrift stores.

---

[38] Gaines, Joanna. *Homebody*, HarperCollins, 2018

Searching for collections of milk glass, toll trays, and needlepoint floral framed art helped me decompress. Making your house a home will help you protect your peace.

Kate Hudson is an entrepreneur, actress, author, and singer. She rose to fame in *Almost Famous*—which is my favorite movie—and earned her a Golden Globe Award. She has become a prominent influencer in the fashion and lifestyle industry and also has a podcast. I love watching her pivot and follow her passions. She has had several husbands and is not afraid to make bold changes in her life and career to follow her passions and then promote them with social media channels. Family is important to her, and her personal brand revolves around authenticity and encouraging others to live well-balanced lives through healthy living and prioritizing balance. She co-hosts her podcast, *Sibling Revelry*, with her brother, Oliver Hudson, and explores family and sibling dynamics with other celebrity siblings. Kate Hudson's recent reinvention is as a songwriter and record producer. She was fearful of this rebrand. However, "after pouring her heart and soul into her album, Hudson is starting this next chapter with confidence."[39] Her entire brand centers on family, support, and finding your Zen.

I mentioned earlier how businesswomen Clea Shearer and Joanna Teplin have influenced me with their book, TV show, and also their brand, The Home Edit. I love nothing more than the Container Store, organization, and cleaning out a good, crowded junk drawer or a bathroom cabinet. For some reason, when my life feels out of control,

---

[39] Nelson, Jeff. "Why Kate Hudson Was 'Afraid' to Pursue Lifelong Music Dream: 'I'm Just Going to Do It,'" *People Magazine*, May 27, 2024

organizing my pantry grounds me, recenters my energy, and allows me to focus and clear my head. The simple task of putting similar items together helps me figure out business with a clear mind and a calm soul. Home Edit is a great brand, and the name is key and so on-brand for them. How can you name your own brand or company? When I am looking to name a brand, company, or new venture, I think of nothing but that brand. I live, sleep, dream, and think of nothing but that name or brand for days.

As much as it helps to know what influences you, it is also important to know what you do not want your brand to reflect. Some influencers now focus intensely on outer beauty. My focus is on beauty on the inside and how to help all of you find your *why* in this confusing time where media comes at you at a record pace, and you must discern what content you want to retain and what content you want to forget. Do not mistake this to mean that looking good on the outside is not on brand for me. I also want to be fashionable and keep current with trends in both beauty and fashion. I believe that you need to dress for success. Keeping your wardrobe current helps us age gracefully and feel good about ourselves and our appearance. However, I do not want the entire brand to be focused on outer beauty. We all know that beauty fades, and what we are left with is what is on the inside. Health, wellness, and inner strength will allow your outer beauty to radiate. The brands I love are timeless and classic versus trendy and superficial.

Your brand should be an extension of who you are and reflect your personal passions. As a businesswoman and mother, separating what you do at home from what you do at work will create a chasm that may make it difficult for you to grow and build your business. If one major part of your *why* and your life is missing from your brand, the brand will lack the depth and character it needs to thrive. That is why my go-to influencers have successful brands they launched collaboratively with other endeavors. They give their audience what they want. They are vulnerable and authentic; they tie their personal lives into their stories and share with the public, their readers, and viewers enough of their homes, lives, recipes, and passions so we can feel like we know them. Their stories are woven into the brands. Kate's love for fitness, yoga, meditation, healthy recipes, and Zen has resulted in her workout clothing line. Reese's love of reading resulted in her book and book club, and Joanna Gaines' passion for home décor and cooking has turned her life itself into a multi-million-dollar lifestyle business.

Fast forward to my current career as a social media curator, podcaster, writer, and consultant—I have figured out a way to monetize what my passions are. What are your values? Take out a notebook or your computer and make lists of things that you love. What activities or hobbies do you engage in? Does listening to music, talking to other business owners, planning events and parties, and spending time with friends work for you? Next, look at the list and see if you can find some kind of pattern. For me, I knew that marketing was my passion. In fact, I should have gone to business school instead of law school. I love music, reading, writing, poetry, and art. Social media and marketing consulting is a perfect way for me to find, utilize, and monetize my passion. Also, it helps to listen to the feedback your friends, colleagues, and others offer you and to ask them what they think your superpowers are.

A personality test can help you hone in on your superpowers. I have taken many tests, including Print, Colby, the Myers-Briggs Type Indicator, and the DISC Assessment. Through these tests and my work with several business coaches, I have learned how to regulate my personality and how to harness my strengths to succeed in both life and work. I have found in my life and career that when one leans fully into his or her superpower, greatness is found. Whether you are a business owner, a leader, or an entrepreneur who is starting a company, if you do not have a passion for what you are doing, if you do not know your *why*, and if you do not love what you are doing, you will not find success and will not be fulfilled.

Use your life experiences, hobbies, and interests to build your own brand effectively. Attitude is all in the gratitude and having appreciation for where you have been, the mistakes you have made along the way, and what you are currently grateful for will all assist your brand in making its debut. The list I made for my personal brand was as follows:

Home décor, accessories, French country, country music, antique stores, flea markets, casseroles, family gatherings around the fireplace, music, tea parties, floral porcelain china, cheerful bright sunrooms, tea with milk and sugar, reading, dance, beaches, beautiful sunrises, nature photos, romantic comedies. Photography has always been my passion, especially black and white photos with a pop of pastel color mixed in, as well as anything French or old European doors. Salty, not sweet. Chicken pot pie. Music documentaries. Acoustic guitar. Lyrics.

This was the list that I made when coming up with my own personal brand. When we worked on my social brand, it was important that it reflected my passions. The muted colors and quotes, as well as beaches, sunsets, and fonts in script mixed with bolder type, all created a calming brand experience. Diving into the social media world with quotes and authenticity was where I was always meant to be. When you know, you just know. If the brand does not feel authentic and you do not feel on point, then you probably are not in the right field. Do more research until you feel that you are living your truth and speaking on brand.

A true entrepreneur lies in bed and brainstorms business ideas that float through her head like the clouds floated above me when I was a little girl. Storytelling, authenticity, and connection are what we crave in this society. A true brand will live in the future if the story behind the brand is articulated properly and people believe in the authenticity of the person behind it. My new company is a consultancy business for branding that has a heavy focus on social media for executives and lawyers who want to highlight their accomplishments, archive their legacies, and build their brands. I truly enjoy speaking with my clients and learning about their *why*, as well as the story behind their brands and businesses.

Once you have the social media profiles up and your website complete, it is time to debut the brand. It is crucial to put out a significant amount of content. Gary Vaynerchuk's book, *Day Trading Attention: How to Actually Build Brand and Sales in the New Social Media World,*[40]

---

[40] Vaynerchuk, Gary. *Day Trading Attention: How to Actually Build Brand and Sales in the New Social Media World*, Harper Business, 2024

is a must-read. The content you share needs to be constant, consistent, and highly relevant to your audience. According to Vaynerchuk, "Everyone is competing for the same, limited space in the user's feed, and the best way to win that space is by making more relevant content." Although most people think that the most important thing about social media is the people who follow you, it is actually about the content itself and how creative it is. Share constant content consistently to build an authentic presence. By sharing your thoughts on these platforms, you will build an audience, and over time, this should increase your profitability by increasing your engagement. Also, both quality and quantity of content are important.

By collaborating with other businesses and starting an online community of like-minded individuals, you can network while still at home in your pajamas. Use your social media to drive traffic to your engine. Your engine is your website, which should also reflect your brand. Your social platforms will be interactive ways to showcase your products, brand, or services. Engagement will be immediate as you drive traffic through hitting the algorithms. Your platforms will garner feedback from potential clients through the comments and engagement you receive. You can build loyalty and trust and create depth in your marketing strategy by inspiring others. Once you build your audience organically, you can then pivot to paid marketing. Experiment with different types of content and then review what worked and did not work so you can understand the platform's success. Following competitors and trends will help you keep current with the marketplace and will drive traffic. You will build credibility and achieve your goals while journaling on all channels.

Another key component of your new brand is finding the quiet white space in the industry you want to enter. What could you do to enhance and improve something that already exists? What can you do to create, inspire, encourage, or promote an improvement to an existing brand? Regroup. Recharge. Unwind. Although those words sound like you are going backward, you are actually moving forward. By taking time off and clearing your mind, entering a new time zone, eating new foods, meeting new people, wining, dining, and resting, you will end up recharging the creative juices that will then allow you to get to the next level with your business or brand.

A true brand will also contribute to society, and you need to ask yourself what you will contribute to society. Lawthentic Consulting is about archiving the legacies of famous lawyers, which is so perfect for me. Sifting through people's old dishes, antique stores, photos, record albums, and discarded memories has always been calming for me. Now, when I think of my antiquing hobby, I can see that it ties into my storytelling business. Marketing and promoting successful lawyers or executives who are also parents syncs with my passion for going back in time and wondering about the stories of the people who left their material goods for me to touch, hold, and purchase. Collecting items, displaying them, and bringing them into tablescapes is analogous to me archiving the legacies of lawyers. Later in life, the daughter of my client, Troy Rafferty, will look back at his legacy and see him as a person and an influencer and not just a bio on a website or the lawyer who made headlines and championed the fight against opiate addiction. She will read about his favorite book, see his personal mantras, and read his original quotes.

The more I tie my personal hobbies, interests, photos, and passions to what I love and what I do, the more this all makes sense. The fabric of my life is like the quilt I made as a Girl Scout Brownie in the first grade. This tapestry connects the elements of a well-lived life into a business brand that highlights what I am most passionate about. Realizing that I am attracted to personal brands and businesses that mimic my own passions, family values, and ambitions has made me understand that doing these exercises will help you launch your brand with authenticity. If you take the time to do the work, the business and the brand will evolve.

Legacies are built with action,
focus, and giving back.

When you google yourself, what do you find? Can you be googled, or are you not populating the internet? It is time to let go. Legacies are built with actions, focus, and giving back. You cannot create a persona until you are that person. Be authentic, and all other clutter will fade into oblivion. Find inner peace and inner beauty, and work on calming your mind and body. I want to bring back that simple abundance and celebrate motherhood and domesticity in conjunction with work. Multitasking is an option if it is handled with precision and care. Branding will help you find your *why*. Your brand is everything. Personal branding is just as important as product or service professional branding. What sets apart a company that goes viral from a company that fails? It is often the branding; people want to follow a person more than they want to follow a product or company. You may have an incredible and innovative product or a service that is important and game-changing. Create a strong personal brand to scale the business to the next level.

Top 5 Ways to Develop and Create a Personal Brand:

1. Make a list of your passions.
2. Be authentic.
3. Find influencers and celebrities who you admire and follow and study their brands.
4. Tie your personal hobbies, passions, and interests to your branding.
5. Create a brand that will contribute to society and find the white space in the industry.

CONCLUSION

> "At the end of the day, it is not your work that you will be most proud of; your children are your greatest accomplishments. Put the time into your family, and greatness will be achieved."

Thank you for coming on this journey with me. I truly hope I have sparked something within you. Regardless of the stage of life you are in, I hope you find your purpose, live authentically, and enjoy a balance between work and family. If you are starting on the journey in the early stages of your career or your family, I hope this book helps you form habits and self-care to allow you to have a healthy mindset and lifestyle necessary to navigate the next phases of your life. If you are struggling in your marriage, I hope this book will offer helpful insights into the various theories of communication you can use to strengthen and work on your relationship. If you cannot work collaboratively on your marriage, you can use this book as a stepping stone to unravel and rebuild your life. If you are contemplating divorce, I hope you gain clarity to move on and find joy and purpose again without worrying about stigma and shame. If you decide to divorce and move on, my wish is for you to see this time as liberating and separate in an authentic and purposeful way. If you are in the "prime time" of your life, I am optimistic that by reinventing yourself, you can look at midlife and an empty nest as an exciting time of renewal and reinvention instead of a crisis or syndrome. This book can guide you to let go of your adult children so you can move forward in a loving way while forming a new kind of mature relationship with them.

If, at any stage of your journey, you need advice and want to build your own business or personal brand, this book will give you the blueprint to get started. I hope I sparked passion in you and gave you the confidence to know that you can make anything in your life happen. Looking back at your life will help you assess your experiences and build a new brand for yourself while archiving your legacy.

Do not beat yourself up when everything falls apart. Each day cannot be perfect. Remember, when everything seems to be falling apart, it's often actually coming together. With an organization system, a plan, lots of laughter, and self-love, you can create the life that you want. It will take work; it will not be easy, and you will fall and fail at times. If you can journal along the way, create a support network, and laugh a lot, then my story is a success. Do not let others dictate your decisions. Follow your inner voice and lead with this intuition regarding the decisions you make, even when those decisions relate to your marriage or your career path. Finally, keep your life and your home organized so you will have more time to spend with your family and friends.

Life can often get in your way. I have had significant personal challenges during my "prime time" and Lawthentic Consulting stage, such as caring for my father. I was fortunate to have a brother and sister who live close by and who are my best friends, my biggest cheerleaders, and have helped me through the most challenging times as we lost our father. However, it is okay to not always meet your goals as long as you continue to keep picking up that manuscript, chip away at your business idea, and keep moving. Your family will always need to come first. Spreading myself too thin resulted in a massive crack in the foundation of our family and was one of the greatest challenges of my life. We all worked through it, though. After getting divorced and leaving my job, I was able to create a healthy life in which I feel fulfilled.

The road map for a truly impactful, meaningful career and life path often has significant hardships along the way. Trust your instincts, and surround yourself with mentors, friends, and family who can listen to you when you have to make difficult decisions. When something feels bad, it is bad. Let it go. Let him go. Move on. Move fast. Make it all happen and work on your mindset to keep moving with positive thoughts, which will lead to positive decisions and result in success and happiness. Do things that get you out of your comfort zone. Take more calculated risks; I am not talking about bungee jumping or climbing Mount Kilimanjaro. Take risks to help you find your passion. For me, getting out of my comfort zone meant launching a podcast, writing this book, and starting a new business in a completely different space. Let's write your story together, find your voice, reinvent you, and find your most authentic life.

On the path to this new you, fear will definitely creep in. When starting all of my companies, I had a "success-only" mindset. If I contemplated failure, I pivoted immediately to add another business line or figured out a way to take a different path to success. Positive thoughts yield successful results, and you can make your life what you manifest. Fear will occasionally creep in, and the people who are paralyzed from following their dreams, finding a life partner who fulfills them, and starting their own businesses will allow fear and negative thinking to dominate their mindset. Failure, for me, is not and was not an option. Complacency will not allow room for creativity; when you are complacent, you cannot grow and cannot get to the next level in life or business. It is important to note that success is not to be measured by monetary gain, fame, or work. Success should be measured by how you structure your life, the friends surrounding you, your relationships, your marriage, and the children you raise. Success should also be evaluated by how you feel in your life. An unhappy homemaker is no different from an unhappy CEO.

What does **make it happen** mean? Does it mean that you will do anything at any cost to make something come to fruition? Does it mean that you will put in the sleepless nights and long days to pursue your dreams? For me, "making it happen" means that if you believe in something and you work hard and set your mind to accomplish something, you have complete power to manifest and **make it happen**. When you have this kind of positive mindset, I believe that anything is possible.

However, setting small, reasonable, and attainable goals and forming small, daily habits will help you reach your goals. It is also imperative to make your dreams realistic and to know when to change course or pivot to make your goals happen.

I try my best to be a good example. This does not mean that I always make the right choices or that I do not make mistakes. We are all human, and we cannot truly find the meaning of success unless we fail or fall down. Own up to your mistakes and then explain the mistakes to your children. I have become more self-aware over the years; I understand myself—my foibles—and I can also work on elements of my personality that need improvement. I have been a work in progress and have used my mistakes and my struggles to become a better person along the way.

It takes years to work through some of our childhood trauma with therapy and introspection. Writing this book has been cathartic. What is your story? Why not start journaling now? You, too, can write your story and later look back at a life well-lived. Journaling your story can help you with both your personal and your professional life. A journal will help your personal brand come to life. Of course, we all make mistakes and the way you can move forward is by learning from them. I think of life as a journey with people who come into your life to teach you lessons. Some people bring negative energy to your life, and if you follow your gut, you will eventually be able to sense that like attracts like. Eliminating toxic people from your life is a skill to be mastered. I am so blessed to have a really great family and friends. They enhance my life with their own stories of adversity and resilience, and they make me laugh even when faced with hardships.

When my mother's Harvard fifty-year reunion book was published, the women were asked to recite and recount their greatest accomplishments. I perused the book and read about famous women who were scientists, lawyers, and doctors who changed the medical, political, and legal landscape. I wondered what my mom would write. Reading her chapter caught my breath as she stated that "my greatest accomplishment in life is my three children and my grandchildren, of whom I am very proud." At the end of the day, it will not be writing a book or starting companies that will be my claim to fame. It is my children, stepchildren, future grandchildren, and husband who mean the most to me. Having my sister, Jennifer, close by and as a mentor and best friend makes each day exponentially better. My family is my greatest accomplishment and brings me the most joy.

Through research for this book, I have become more self-aware and emotionally intelligent. Understanding what truly matters in life makes this book even more important. If you can define the kind of parenting style you want to have, work on your marriage, find time to connect with your spouse, enjoy your friends, and find the balance in your life while still bringing your best self to work, you will have achieved ultimate success.

My Affirmations

- If it was that easy, everyone would do it.
- Surround yourself with people who push you outside your comfort zone.
- Authenticity is everything.
- Follow your dreams, your truth, and your inner voice.
- Hire slow, fire fast.
- Accountability is key.
- Daily affirmations lead to success in both life and work.
- Never stop learning. It keeps you young.
- Find your passion and then promote and publicize it.
- Feel your feelings.
- Laugh often and a lot.
- Coffee and sleep are everything.
- Gratitude is in your attitude.

"At the end of the day, it is not your work that you will be most proud of; your children are your greatest accomplishments. Put the time into your family, and greatness will be achieved."

THANK YOU FOR READING MY BOOK!

LET'S CONNECT!

To continue the conversation and connect with me,

SCAN THE QR CODES

@elizabethmagazineesq **LawthenticConsulting.com**

I appreciate your interest in my book and value your feedback as it helps me improve future versions of this book. I would appreciate it if you could leave your invaluable review on Amazon.com with your feedback. Thank you!